Finding Jesus on the Metro

Finding Jesus on the Metro

And Other Surprises Doing Church in a New Day

PAUL NIXON

The Pilgrim Press
Cleveland

ALL THE SERVANTS OF GOD WHO LOVE PEOPLE
MORE THAN TRADITION, YOU WHO ARE OPEN TO
DISCOVER JESUS IN NEW AND UNEXPECTED PLACES.

SFI CERTIFIED SOURCING

FIBER USED IN THIS PRODUCT LINE
MEETS THE SOURCING REQUIREMENTS
OF THE SFI PROGRAM
WWW.SFIPROGRAM.ORG

The Pilgrim Press, 700 Prospect Avenue, Cleveland, Ohio 44115
thepilgrimpress.com
© 2009 by Paul Nixon

Scripture quotations, unless otherwise noted, are from the New Revised
Standard Version of the Bible, ©1989 by the Division of Christian Education
of the National Council of Churches of Christ in the United States of America
and are used by permission. Changes have been made for inclusivity.

13   12   11   10   09   5   4   3   2   1

Library of Congress Cataloging-in-Publication Data

Nixon, Paul, 1962–
    Finding Jesus on the Metro : and other surprises doing church in a
new day / Paul Nixon.
        p. cm.
    ISBN 978-0-8298-1854-3
    1. Pastoral theology—United States.   I. Title.
BV4011.3.N58 2009
253—dc22   2008053837

Contents

INTRODUCTION . . . VII

PART ONE AWAKENING TO A NEW DAY

1   Every Neighborhood Is Now a Changing Neighborhood . . . 3

2   Yes, Christendom Really Did Die . . . 8

3   Buddha Is Not Our Enemy: Cheap Consumerism Is . . . 14

4   We Are So Incredibly Busy . . . 21

5   We Are Desperate for Authentic Community . . . 27

6   Families Have Never Come in More Flavors . . . 35

7   We May Be Raising a Generation of Heroes . . . 41

8   We Have Mastered the Art of Compartmentalizing . . . 46

PART TWO THE ONLY THING CERTAIN IS THE JOURNEY

9   My Journey to the City . . . 55

10   Getting Unsettled . . . 63

11   Who Said It Would Be Easy? . . . 69

12   Lessons from the Underground Railroad . . . 74

13   Discovering the Back Side of the Mountain . . . 83

14   Honoring the People You Meet along the Journey . . . 90

15   Paying Attention to the Power of Tribe . . . 98

16   Giving the World Something Better . . . 105
     Than More Church People

17   Staying in Touch with God's Call . . . 113

18   Trusting God through It All . . . 121

     EPILOGUE . . . 127

Introduction

THIS IS A BOOK ABOUT THE SPIRITUAL JOURNEY OF CHRISTIAN ministry in twenty-first-century America. Having experienced life firsthand in vibrant congregations in four different decades, I confess that my fifth decade is a bit disorienting. Although much of what we have learned regarding effective ministry is still true after all these years, there is also much that is changing. And given the pace of the change, especially the tectonic shifts in Americans' relationship to organized religion, we have little idea what great ministry may look like ten or twenty years hence.

Faithful service to God in this era means, in large part, being good learners. Being a good learner entails paying close attention to the changing needs, thoughts, and values of the people we intend to serve. In addition, through trial and error, good ministry learners apply accumulated spiritual and ministry wisdom to these new challenges. We can learn as much from our disappointments as from our successes.

Faithfulness also means that a steady practice of prayer is our lifeline. It means that we may often try things that just don't work. It means that we may relate more closely to the experience of the apostles in the book of Acts, experiencing hardship and resistance, than to the experience of Reverend Whoever, who is the latest to tout ten ways to build a megachurch in Orlando.

While evangelical megachurches will be with us for the foreseeable future, there is good evidence to suggest that they will play an increasingly marginal role in our society. Even now, they involve a small and shrinking fraction of the overall population. Very few of their members are converts from outside the Christian tradition. Their influence in public policy is waning. And the majority of their adult children are now leaving organized churches nearly as fast as the children of mainline Protestants, even if they may remain engaged with Christian spirituality in certain ways. We are living into a century when all forms of highly institutionalized Christianity (liberal, conservative, Pentecostal, and otherwise) are steadily diminishing in American life. The statistical evidence is clear.[1]

The first section of this book explores eight ways in which the context of Christian ministry is changing in North America. Every church needs to awaken to these eight realities of the world it is seeking to serve. The land is shifting beneath us as we walk.

The latter section of the book explores what it means to be on a ministry journey in such a time as this. You will be invited to consider your own journey and the journey of your congregation.

Beyond understanding the world better, and even beyond figuring out effective ministry strategies for new situations, we do well to remember that we are on a spiritual journey with God! In every era, regardless of how valiantly we succeed or fail in the tasks of sharing Christ's good news, extending social justice, and building vibrant faith communities, *we who come together as church*

---

1. The statistical evidence on the demise of mainline Protestantism is so well documented now that it is old news. The best summary of the statistical evidence for evangelical decline that I have found is journalist Christine Wicker's book *The Fall of the Evangelical Nation* (New York: Harper One, 2008).

share in a holy journey. On this journey, God treasures our faithfulness more than our accomplishments. We are journeying with God into unknown territory, just like Abraham did. We remember and celebrate Abraham for his faithfulness—*and for God's faithfulness to him*—not for any particular personal accomplishments that he achieved apart from God.

The theme of journey is sometimes overlooked in the task of congregational development. We latch onto the models of what worked somewhere in the 1990s and push, push, push for fast results—forgetting that we are first and foremost people on a spiritual journey with God. If we are faithful in following where God leads (if we seek first God's realm . . .) all the other concerns tend to work themselves out (all these other things are added unto us). On such a journey with God, it should be no surprise if we stumble onto a new and perhaps revolutionary way of appropriating the Christian faith tradition in community. If we are living in the book of Acts, we live in the holy suspense of "What next?" We live trusting that God is still writing an amazing story.

I have written these pages from an urban perspective, thanks to my recent experiences serving in the Washington, D.C., area. This book is colored by the spirituality of that city, as well as by the baffling challenges and abundant blessings of urban ministry. Cities have been setting the pace for culture for several millennia now. If you live in a small town or a relatively homogeneous suburban community, some of the observations in this book may not yet ring true for the place where you live. *However, there is a good chance that what we are learning in the city today will be profoundly relevant to your suburban or village church tomorrow as cultural shifts ripple out across the land.* One reason why my city may have relevance to yours in the days ahead is because so many of the people in central D.C. are twenty-somethings. Many of these will soon marry and move from the world of loft condos to a home with a yard and a decent school nearby—maybe in a neighborhood near you.

In a homogeneous community, the vast majority of people are of one ethnic group, speak one common language, and probably share a wide array of common cultural touch points. We see homogeneous enclaves in all kinds of settings, ranging from urban Chinatowns to retirement villages that are 95 percent Anglo. Church development tends to be easier in such settings since a very high percentage of folks can be served with a single ministry strategy and approach. However, the United States is rapidly becoming more heterogeneous or varied. Go shopping at Target on a Saturday morning in formerly all-white suburbs outside Houston or on Long Island, and you may feel like you are at the United Nations.

Those of us who minister to the newest generation of adults, or to highly educated adults, or to communities of extreme diversity, or to those folks who live outside the assumption that Christianity is the world's spiritual norm, often have a very different experience from our colleagues who serve congregations in the American heartland. I spent many years in that heartland, particularly in so-called red (Republican, or conservative) states. Though I now work in decidedly blue (Democrat, or liberal) territory, I still coach churches in the heartland, and I see that even in these areas American adults are steadily slipping from the orbit of the institutional church.

Sometimes those of us working the blue regions are perceived by our Southern and Midwestern colleagues as "struggling" in ministry because our ministry fields are so complex, our facilities are often so very old and needy, and the sizes of our flocks are typically only a fraction of the number we would have out in the Atlanta exurbs loaded with two-adult households, raising kids. Our work may sometimes feel harder in the blue zone, but it is important work because our churches often work in the midst of significant diversity, often at the nexus of faith and emerging culture.

The faithful and tenacious congregation of seventy-five people in a cavernous sanctuary so recently full to the rafters is quickly becoming as common in suburbia as it is downtown. Times they are a'changin'—and fast! The sooner your church understands these changes, the better the chances you will live to serve another day. Some who serve in our cities manage to connect with human hurts and hopes in amazing ways. A few have built large congregations of urban poor folks, evangelical young adults, or LGBT (lesbian, gay, bisexual, transgendered) folks, rarely without some controversy and effort to color outside certain lines of propriety observed by the culturally homogeneous suburban church. I want to celebrate such victories. But I also want to acknowledge that most twenty-first-century churches will gather fewer than a hundred people on Sunday. In many cases, these smaller churches will bring an excellence of ministry practice and specialization in serving certain populations that will exceed that of their megachurch neighbors. In God's economy, it takes all of us!

Much of the wisdom that is passed along about church development and leadership these days comes from the suburban context, and much of it grows from ministry experience that is at least a decade out of date. Urban church leaders, rural church leaders, small church leaders, and theological progressives sometimes want to throw those books in the river because so many of the models, so many of the principles, so many of the values simply do not translate to our context. As a result of this frustration and disconnect, many folks tuned out of the church development conversation years ago. Consequently, many churches are now a bit behind the curve in terms of some best practices that could really help them in their work.

I have received gracious feedback from both urban and rural church leaders to my last book, *I Refuse to Lead a Dying Church*. I am glad that so many have found it helpful and encouraging. Any leader or group that will profit from this book will also profit from that one. This book is a sequel to *I Refuse*. It picks up the conversation where that book concluded, moving beyond a few simple, positive, and proactive ministry choices to consider how the journey ahead for most churches may be very different than the one we know from days gone by.

Finding Jesus on the Metro is not a ministry *how-to* book. It might belong in the category of a *helpful-clues* book. In the world unfolding before us, we are scrambling to deal not only with unprecedented diversity of people, but also with the cutting edge of rapidly changing attitudes toward organized religion. In the midst of such seismic shifts, helpful clues are the best I can offer.

I bring to these pages an underlying assumption that *faithfulness* (a clearly biblical value) is more fundamental than outward *success* (a more secular value). I do not subscribe to the idea that faithfulness and success are mutually exclusive. I simply believe faithfulness should be our primary focus, and that we should trust God to bring success in the mission.

My goal for this book is to provoke helpful thinking, praying, and conversing prior to major decision making about your church's ministry and future. Throughout the book, you will find sections labeled **MINISTRY CLUE**, relating the material in that section to your church's life and work.

MINISTRY CLUE

A downloadable study guide is available for groups of church leaders who wish to study this book together in either a three- or five-session format. This study guide is available at www.epicentergroup.org. Such a study often serves as a helpful primer preceding a ministry planning process or season of major decision-making. Before a group of people can make good decisions together, it helps if they can gather to explore key issues and ask the right questions together.

■ ■ ■

We are entering an era in the journey of the church when we are called anew to walk by faith. James Forbes, pastor emeritus of the Riverside Church in New York City, calls a time such as this "the night season."[2] It is an era when the way is not clear, certainly not as clear for ministry leaders in the city as for leaders in suburbia, not as clear for any of us as may have been the case for our predecessors a couple of generations ago. Each new generation creates new puzzles for established congregations. However, we currently face more puzzles than at any time I can remember. My work in the suburban South of the 1990s was like summer in the Yukon compared to now.

And yet, God created a world where we all live exactly half our lives in the night, during which we can't see as clearly as during the day. There is nothing evil or wrong with those seasons in ministry when the way is not clear. Those seasons are just another part of life.

Indeed, the whole book of Acts was written in a night season, when much was unclear. Those apostles who look so sure of themselves in history's rear view mirror were actually flying by the seat of their pants most of the time in the first century! And they discovered that the night season may be when we experience God's very best work.

In the night season:

- If you are part of an established church anywhere in North America, you are probably discovering that the ministry practices that worked well only a decade ago are now not nearly as effective.

- If you are new to church leadership, perhaps just hitting the streets post-seminary, guess what? The church that formed you spiritually is now fast passing away; and the church that you will lead may look little like the one that formed you!

---

2. This term is from a sermon James Forbes preached at Shiloh Baptist Church in Washington, D.C., on the second Sunday of Easter, 2008.

- If you are part of an established church in the central city or the open country, the chances are good that far fewer people are attaching to your church than would be the case if you were serving a church in a homogeneous middle-class suburb. However, your church may have beat the odds simply by still having its doors open, while many others around it have either relocated or gone out of business. Many of our long-established urban and rural churches are tenacious, vibrant communities, on the cusp of new life. Others are nearing the end of their lives and looking for ways to bequeath their spiritual legacy to another group who will carry on in the same place for years to come.

If your congregation is seeking to stay relevant to your community in this new era, I want to encourage you to hang in there! Keep praying, keep learning, keep innovating, keep loving, keep serving, keep dreaming! The people of your community need you and the ministry of your church, both now and for the long run.

Part One

A W A K E N I N G   T O   A   N E W   D A Y

1

EVERY NEIGHBORHOOD IS NOW A CHANGING NEIGHBORHOOD

I REMEMBER A TIME, EXTENDING FROM 1968 UNTIL I GRADUATED high school in 1980, when my family lived in new neighborhoods where every house was inhabited by a family that had either built it or bought it new. Twice we moved into brand new houses ourselves. Twice we were the second owners. The churches in our neighborhoods thrived, populated largely by a homogeneous community of Anglo homeowners with stay-at-home moms and station wagons full of kids.

Some of my favorite childhood memories are of playing in someone else's house, under construction, in the weeks before the house was sealed from the outside. My friends and I would run up and down stairs that had no banisters, imagining that the house was our castle or our starship. My Brittany spaniel, Happy, would often run with us through the house. We gave each room an identity. For example, if we were traveling through space, for some reason the kitchen always became the cockpit. Maybe this was because most of us watched our mothers run our respective worlds from the kitchen. The sweet smell of sawdust still elicits happy memories for me. This was American suburbia in its glory years.

In the years after World War II, American suburbs exploded with the advent of the fifteen-year mortgage, and then the thirty-year, and then the adjustable-rate, no-interest, no-money-down mortgage. Suddenly, a new generation of homes came on line from coast to coast outfitted with the latest home technologies, priced so we could move in. People often think "white flight" from the central city was simply about racism. True, it was in part a flight from persons who were different. But it was also a flight to these incredible modern houses filled with the intoxicating scent of new shag carpet and also to the brand new air conditioned schools just down the street.

Millions of American kids still grow up in such places. There are neighborhoods of tract homes in southern California today where one would never have imagined human habitation thirty years ago. Brand new cities. We used to go camping near Temecula, California, in a region that felt like the wilderness described in Exodus. Where we pitched our pup tent then could very possibly be a Starbucks parking lot today.

My mother still lives on the edge of suburban development, in a neighborhood across the street from a brand new shopping mall. She and my father were the first residents of that house. Some of her neighbors are the originals too. This is classic suburbia: a first generation, culturally homogeneous bedroom community not far from a larger, older city core.

When I was a kid, suburbia was considered to be in contrast to the "changing community," the neighborhoods closer to the city core that had an older housing stock, where families with less money—sometimes immigrant families—moved in, changing the face and feel of the older neighborhoods in amazing ways. In fact, the changing community often quickly became a homogeneous community all over again, simply with a different group of people, who in turn created new community institutions and churches.

Homogeneous communities in America have a robust history of church development. We can trace them all the way back to the

Puritans and Congregationalists who settled the Massachusetts Bay Colony, then to the proliferation of Catholic parishes in the late 1800s with the massive wave of central European immigrants to North America, to the spread of Methodist churches all across the continent (thanks to circuit riders who greeted the largely Anglo westward pioneers claiming their homesteads in Kansas and beyond), then (in the years of my childhood) to the proliferation of new neighborhood churches in the post–World War II suburban communities, and, more recently still, to the birth of large Korean churches in many American cities.

But there are not many Puritans left in Massachusetts, or Roman Catholics in inner-city Cincinnati, or Methodists in Denver, or liberal white Protestants in Anaheim. Even among the Koreans, their newest generations are marrying into the broader culture and drifting from the historic churches that so recently were cornerstones of Korean culture in North America. One result of all this is that many once thriving churches have faded. Many have died. In each of the neighborhoods where I grew up, the churches have been challenged. The majority of those churches have much older congregations now, struggling to relate effectively to the new families moving in as their neighbors. When we remember that almost all the parishes that the apostles planted in Turkey and Europe also evaporated long ago, we realize this shift is not unique to our time or to North America. Communities change, and community-based churches adapt, relocate, or fade away.

There are Southern Baptist churches in south Dallas County, Texas, that have relocated three times in half a century, due to the rapid expansion of the African American and Hispanic communities in a vast, formerly white middle-class section of Dallas. New megachurches have grown up in their wake, serving well the people of color in south Dallas. In Washington, D.C., formerly black majority neighborhoods are now home to growing Anglo, Hispanic, and Asian populations, resulting in shrinking, aging black congregations, following patterns similar to what white congregations may have experienced in the same neighborhoods fifty years ago. The two fastest growing congregations in downtown Washington in the last decade have been majority Anglo new church starts.

I have studied demographic reports on hundreds of American communities as I have consulted with congregations in those places. Roughly three out of four of those communities are dealing with significant issues of social change due to migration: ethnic and cultural groups moving in and out of geographical territory.

But now, layer in another dimension of change: call it generational. There is a never-ending rise of new adults within these groups, who think and act differently from their parents. When you consider how fast and vast the changes are that we're now experiencing from one generation to the next, you will quickly see that almost every community could now be called a "changing community."

We will talk more about generational change later in this book. But for now, hold on to two thoughts:

- Currently almost every community in America could accurately be labeled a "changing community."
- In a changing community, churches simply cannot continue to do what they have always done and expect to exist for long. Churches with a good future in this new century can expect to live in constant learning mode about new ways to do ministry.

Think about the community where your church's facility is located. Most regional denominational offices have access to demographic studies for your community. Contact them to get hold of such a report, so that you can take a close look at your area's objective reality. Demographic studies are like eyeglasses that enable us to see more accurately what we otherwise filter and distort through our memories, our emotions, and our denial. So with or without a demographic report, think about your church's community:

- Who settled this community originally?
- How many major population shifts have there been so far? Who moved in? When did these occur?
- Who were the people who originally settled your church?
- How has your church adapted to the social changes in the community?
- Is the current generation of young adults with kids relating to your church's ministry? If so, why? If not, why not?
- Do you care enough about the people around you to make some internal sacrifices and changes in order to connect with and serve those folks more effectively? (Notice that I am asking if you care, not if your church cares.)
- Do you care enough about the people of your community to become an advocate for helpful change and new kinds of ministry? Will you stand toe to toe with those in your church who might not be focused on the Great Commission or the imperative to serve the community?

Every neighborhood is now a changing neighborhood, including yours. Wise churches see this. And they understand that ministry strategies must evolve if we wish to remain meaningfully connected to our community.

2

Yes, Christendom
Really Did Die

It is almost clichéd now to say that Christendom in most of the United States has died. It kicked the bucket sometime in my childhood while I was playing Star Trek in a house under construction. Believe it or not, in the early twentieth century, Canada had a higher church affiliation than the United States, and so the collapse of the church there has been more spectacular (or disheartening) than anything we have seen in the United States— yet. In Europe, the decline of the church as cultural center happened slowly, across many generations, even centuries. In Canada, the collapse occurred in less than fifty years.

South of the Canadian border, the generational research among the young Americans of the early twenty-first century points to a significant shifting in attitudes related to God and to organized religion, unprecedented in our nation's history.

Ten years ago, I thought that the demise of Christendom in America meant simply that we had moved beyond the illusion that we were in some respect "a Christian nation" when only about a fourth of our people attended any church on a regular basis, and fewer than that practiced Christianity seriously. Now I see far more significant implications of what it means to live in a post-Christian culture. Recent research from the Barna Group indicates that up to 40 percent of young adults now think of themselves as being *other than* Christian, a phenomenal shift in a society in which until recently even agnostics often identified with Christianity in surveys, if only as a way of saying that they tried to live by the Golden Rule. In the new world, 40 percent of our young adults choose not to make that identification at all, up from a negligible percentage a couple decades back.[3] It is certainly imaginable that a generation from now, for the children of these people, that number could go to 70 or 80 percent, similar to what we see in Canada.

If, for example, you take a walk in and out of posh home décor stores on Colorado Boulevard in Pasadena, California, you will notice that there are more decorative Buddhas than decorative crosses for sale on store shelves. Religious trinkets and art may not indicate internal devotion, but I do think they signal that the symbolic centrality of Christianity to our culture is diminishing. Or perhaps you would like to take a virtual walk following the links between Facebook or MySpace pages. If you have young adult children, start with their page and then follow the links to their friends' pages and on to the friends of their friends. In each place, look what they have written in the slot related to religious views, and keep score. Wiccans, Pagans, and Buddhists will probably outnumber UCC people, Episcopalians, Presbyterians, or Disciples of Christ. More commonly, you will see that they make some kind of statement against institutional forms of religion without clearly indicating what they do believe in.

This drop in our culture's casual identification with Christianity may strike you as a terrible loss—but I am more ambiva-

---

3. See the book *Unchristian: What a New Generation Really Thinks about Christianity and Why It Matters* by David Kinnemon and Gabe Lyons (Grand Rapids: Baker Books, 2007). This book, based on research from the Barna Group with young adult Americans, draws conclusions from an evangelical perspective.

lent. I do not think low-impact, Christmas-Easter civic religion ever served us that well. It always seemed to me to be a cheap distortion of Christianity. I am not especially sad to see it departing.

For at least two generations, Christianizing (and possibly drug-proofing) children has been perhaps the number one motivation getting people to start attending Christian churches when their children were between three and seven years of age. In my years as pastor in two very large suburban churches, I watched scores of parents each year affiliate with our church—motivated to get their kids into a quality Christian environment. While this is still a powerful motivation for millions of American families,

---

MINISTRY CLUE

If many parents now perceive the church as one provider of children's activities among many, we would be wise to look for market gaps:

- Is there a type of recreation that is missing from the community options? Some churches have introduced indoor soccer or sports leagues without scorekeeping as a complement to current, often very competitive, community offerings.

- If parents are looking at team sports and disciplined skill development as important pieces of character building, then the church needs to find arts and disciplines it can teach better than anyone else in town.

- As funding for arts education withers in public schools, churches could explore giving music lessons, building jazz bands, and training high quality vocal ensembles both indigenous and classical in style. Or a church could create (or host) a children's theater program committed to high quality performance.

■   ■   ■

there are millions of others for whom it is not a motivation. *Unless we change our classic appeal to parents and families, we can content ourselves with fewer and fewer children in our churches.*

There may always be some secular parents who believe that Christian mythology is as harmless to their children as fairy tales and Santa Claus—just a warm, fuzzy part of growing up. They may see Sunday school as a benign part of socializing small children—perhaps filtered through fond memories of a simpler time in their own lives when they once believed in God. But the urgency of this type of hobby for their children may easily be squeezed out of their schedules, given all the juggling they do with their children's more rigorous extracurricular hobbies, birthday parties, and the multitude of fun things to do on weekends.

If nearly half of the next generation of parents do not see themselves as even marginally Christian, it is a good bet that they will look to many kinds of involvements to help build character in their kids. Most often they turn to team sports and other endeavors that require practice and discipline (dance, piano, gymnastics, for example). Quite frankly, for years most churches have not offered any children's program or endeavor that requires practice, teamwork, or discipline. Church-based children's choir programs once offered that, but in the current cultural climate, only about one in ten girls would tolerate singing in a traditional chorus and maybe one in a hundred boys. There are other more attractive options out there—lots of them!

As the church, we do well to pay close attention to the agendas, the values, and perceived needs of our neighbors. Especially when we are marketing ourselves to the community on our signage, in our community events, in our postcards, and even in our worship services, we must be relevant to people's real life concerns.

When a sign in front of a church building proclaims "Second Sunday of Epiphany" as the top headline, or promotes a sermon topic formed around an institutional or insider agenda ("Remembering What We Believe about Baptism"), we are choosing to speak gibberish to post-Christian people. When the home page of our website spotlights our capital fund-raising program underway, it tells post-Christian people that we are a church intent on finding our way into their pocketbook, so as to build bigger and better monuments. (I ran across a home page the other day that was entirely focused on the fall bake sale. What this told me was that they are a church intent on wasting my energy in frivolous busy-ness.)

Although it's been many years ago now, I will never forget coming home one Sunday afternoon from an esoteric lectionary-driven sermon that I had preached to my congregation about

---

MINISTRY CLUE

If your church continues to use a lectionary of random scriptures selected by a far distant committee and tagged to movements in the liturgical year rather than to movements in the soul of your community, I urge you, at the very least, to do the following:

- Keep a running list of the top ten or fifteen issues (spiritual, social, economic, and so on) that people are facing in your world—and keep your eyes open for every time that a lectionary text speaks to one of these critical life issues. In a post-Christian world, few people are interested in excellent talks on issues that feel irrelevant.

- If the lectionary lends itself to a relevant theme, look for at least one other reading from a nonscriptural source that adds wisdom and clarity to the issue (from literature, from science, from another religion).

- Consider breaking from lectionary preaching every so often to do a series around life issues. American churchgoers really love these.

■   ■   ■

some curious facet of Christian theology only to discover a TV preacher in a nearby city preaching on something relevant: "How to Pray When You Don't Feel Like Praying." He may or may not have been as theologically nuanced as I was, but he sure as heck was talking about something that felt more urgent and interesting. We all crave a deeper spirituality, but most of us have difficulty disciplining ourselves to pray. The preacher nailed the experience of every human being on the planet. He was relevant. That was an "aha" moment for me. I realized that I needed to rethink what was driving my preaching. That was back in the late 1980s when a good chunk of my parishioners still showed up out of Christendom-based duty and loyalty. In the 1990s I abandoned the lectionary and began to preach to the needs of people, still always rooting my preaching in sound biblical exegesis. One result: a very rapidly growing church.

In a post-Christian world, fewer and fewer people will automatically attend our churches or even come church shopping unless an inner crisis propels them through our doors. Fewer and fewer people will tolerate an experience that does not help them feel demonstrably better about life and the challenges before them.

But help me with my life and with my relationships, learn my name before I get out the door, and the chances are good that you will see me again. Go one step further: help me aim my life toward blessing others, and if I am among the youngest of American adults, the chances are even better that you will see me again and again.

Christendom is gone with the wind. But opportunities for relevant ministry are as plentiful as ever—if only we look for them!

3

BUDDHA IS NOT OUR ENEMY:
CHEAP CONSUMERISM IS

I FIRST BECAME ACQUAINTED WITH EASTERN RELIGIONS WHILE I was in college. During the semester that I studied Buddhism and Hinduism, the movie *Gandhi* came out. My roommate and I went to see it. Here was Gandhi, a devout Hindu holy man whose philosophy of nonviolent social change played a significant role in India's struggle for independence from the British. His philosophy was formed in part by the teachings of Jesus, and in turn it formed the foundation for the teachings of Martin Luther King Jr. Yet Gandhi never converted to Christianity in terms of joining a church.

After the movie, my friend and I got into an argument about whether or not Gandhi would be in heaven. For me, not only had the man effectively followed Jesus, but he had lived a life that bore the fruit of the Spirit of God. For my roommate, to think about Gandhi being a part of the community of God's beloved threatened his understanding of both the uniqueness of Jesus and the centrality of the institutional church to God's redemptive work in the world. I viewed Jesus as a window into the life of God and the suffering, sacrificial redemptive love that lies at the heart of God. If another person looked through another window and saw very much the same thing I saw, all the better! What if we Christians were talking about overlapping spiritual realities and approaching the same Divine Mystery as our neighbors, just with different symbols, different names, different cultural histories and different worldviews? Certainly there would be uniqueness in our Christian perspective, but also there would be much common ground with our neighbors and very helpful new insights for us.

My roommate and I cheerfully agreed to disagree. It was a good thing for us to learn how to do.

At times, I listen to people who are within the Christian community and who use the same language and symbols as I do, but with utterly different meanings and spirit. I begin to feel as if I have more in common spiritually with certain non-Christians who are filled with God's love and peace than with fundamentalists who appear to be filled with anger and angst.

I am not the first to feel this way. Why did Martin Luther King Jr. relate so powerfully to Vietnamese Buddhist mystic Thich Nhat Hanh and to the writings of Mahatma Gandhi? What was the Catholic mystic and spiritual giant Thomas Merton doing in India meeting with the Dalai Lama days before his death? Neither King nor Merton was a postmodernist. Each lived deeply in love with Jesus Christ and remained planted squarely within a western faith community. They were simply sensitive spiritual beings who discovered that the Spirit of God is doing amazing work in lives far beyond the bounds of the Christian churches.

Closer to home, all I have to do is observe the joy in the life of the Buddhist woman who cuts my hair. I wish that all the Christians I knew could possess what she has. Sure, I have spiritual treasures to share with her, but she obviously has something special to share in return, something that is not apparent in the lives of many of the Christians in our city.

One of the practices Thich Nhat Hanh teaches is "compassionate listening." This is a practice of intentionally stepping aside from one's own baggage, anxieties, and stubborn convictions and

---

MINISTRY CLUE

Consider ways that you can practice intentional listening with your community, helping you to better understand the people around you and helping them to see that you care about them enough to hush and let them talk.

- Focus groups offer one way to do community listening. Invite twelve people from your neighborhood who are not a part of your church. Expect eight or nine to show up. Plan to feed them well. Have a skilled group facilitator lead a one-hour discussion around varied themes focused on community needs and the needs of "typical" people in the community. Focus on the community, not on the church. Let the people attending coach you and give the church advice. Repeat the process with a second group to test the results.

- Take a community survey in a public place, possibly at a church exhibit at the fair. The point is not advertising what your church *does*, but advertising *that you care*. Focus the survey questions on discovering community needs and showing your interest in neighbors' insights.

■   ■   ■

---

simply listening with the purpose of understanding the other. Stephen Covey taught something very similar in *Seven Habits of Highly Effective People*.[4] Listening is transformational and healing—especially if we allow a person to express to us his or her pain, perceptions, and the ways that he or she has felt wounded or misunderstood by us. If by virtue of centuries-old meditational practices we can chill out enough to hear one another without reacting, what an improved place the world would be. And what amazing

4. Thich Nhat Hahn, *Anger: Wisdom for Cooling the Flames* (New York: Riverhead Books, 2001), 3–4; Stephen Covey, *Seven Habits of Highly Effective People: Restoring the Character Ethic* (New York: Simon and Schuster, 1989).

interfaith dialogue and witness could be possible. If people of faith and communities of faith were to model this, it would be such a helpful gift to this planet. It cuts to the very heart of peacemaking.

Christian churches have a very bad rep with regard to the practice of listening. A few years back, the novel *The Poisonwood Bible* set forth a caricature of organized Christianity, feeding the questionable assumption of many secular people that most pastors and missionaries are bigots and buffoons. Much of what such secular people see on cable television further confirms this stereotype. This is a critical matter for correction if the church is to thrive in twenty-first-century America. How might we convey that millions of persons with religious faith are also humble, kind, funny, and open-minded?

The spirit of our age is very much open to the spiritual wisdom that comes from eastern sources. Some of this wisdom is encased in and connected to worldviews that do not reconcile well with Christianity. Other wisdom traditions (such as Zen) come with minimal metaphysical assumptions and offer methods for peacemaking that can help us live out the Christian value of loving neighbor as self. I find no threat in the latter. Neither do the majority of adults in the new world in which we live.

In the new global village, most people have unprecedented access to ideas and spiritual sources of wisdom and hope. No wonder so many of us are marching to the beat of other drummers. Now even extremely conservative Christians sometimes meditate, practice Yoga, and learn Tai Chi—often at the church's recreation center.

This leaves the church with a choice—we can pursue a line of reasoning that is increasingly silly on its face to millions of young Americans, that Christianity offers the only truth and all these other cultures are spiritually deluded and blind. Or we can take the equally implausible position that all spiritual paths lead to the same place, when clearly they do not. Or we can find a third way—discerning the common ground between the historic world faith communities. Wisdom from one can clarify and help us better to live out our own faith tradition, and to see what our own experience of Christ brings to the table that is truly different from what our neighbors may have experienced in their respective traditions.

MINISTRY CLUE

If you are a pastor, look for opportunities to build a collegial friendship with a clergy leader of another faith group —the further from your tradition, the better. Keep your eyes open to opportunities to allow mixing between the two communities:

- in local mission projects
- in carefully crafted events where each community shares something with the other, a tradition or faith practice that is minimally threatening and easily digestible within the framework of the other faith community
- in shared mealtimes where the best dishes of each culture are shared with the whole group assembled—possibly at Thanksgiving time

■ ■ ■

We Christians can learn much from brilliant writers and practitioners of other religions without in any way diminishing the truth or beauty of our faith. The smart young adults that live around me in Washington totally get this. They know that we don't have to be afraid of Buddha.

A big part of young adults' ambivalence about organized Christianity is that they don't think the church sees what to them is so painfully obvious: that we westerners do not have a corner on truth. Fairly or not, they have equated organized Christianity with chauvinistic exclusivist attitudes toward other cultures. They see Christian chauvinism and exclusivism as doing to spirituality what the United States has so tragically done in foreign policy during the early twenty-first century—saying we are better than everyone else and refusing to dialogue humbly with our neighbors. Most of the people I work with want no part of continued cultural imperialism.

If the church is to regain its respect, we need to communicate a clear and humble sense of:

- who we are
- what our faith community and tradition believe about God
- how we understand the centrality of Jesus in our lives
- how the cosmic Christ transcends the historic Jesus
- how persons in other cultures may at times live more Christ-like lives than we do

What we should fear rather than Buddha is religion reduced to trinkets and stylish icons, or bumper sticker slogans. When holy symbols are valued primarily as fashion statements, simply to be dangled off our rear view mirrors or to adorn our fireplace mantles, something is wrong.

In this multicultural society, we should exercise great care that we do not take such symbols so lightly that we casually mix them a la carte, without any connection to their historical context or the communities that hallowed them.[5] In the world that is coming, there will always be some syncretism and eclectic drawing from multiple faith traditions. But it does not have to be cheap. When in our worship or teaching we draw from ancient or extra-Christian sources, we owe people at least a note of context about the piece of art or music or poetry. Even in a monocultural society, if church and Bible are treated simply as consumer goods to

---

5. This idea is well developed by my fellow Washingtonian, Vincent J. Miller, a professor of theology at Georgetown University, in a book entitled *Consuming Religion: Christian Faith and Practice in Consumer Culture* (New York: Continuum Books, 2005).

be marketed, it is easy to find ourselves suddenly teaching and preaching the great stories or practices of our faith community as therapy for what ails us, so that we may miss the greater points contained by our tradition's great stories. This is a significant matter for our integrity as spiritual leaders.

It is very easy to transform the faith of our community into spiritual potato chips—cheap pragmatic life lessons that taste good and "hit the spot," salted with little tidbits from Eastern practice and American pop psychology. But our potato chips may betray both the sheep we are called to feed and the Christ who calls us to feed them. Some things taste good but have little nutritional value. In seeking to avoid the pothole of irrelevance, we should be careful not to oversteer in the other direction by reducing the faith simply to whatever the consumer desires.

But, in any case, we truly don't have to be afraid of Buddha.

4

We Are So Incredibly Busy

It isn't just a Washington thing. Granted, the D.C. area is the busiest lifestyle I have yet observed on the planet, but busyness is the norm in every corner of North America, not only among parents of small children but even among the small children themselves. People who have no reason to be so busy sometimes run faster than the rest of us—think of today's so-called retirees. What's up with the frenzy of activity that nearly all of us are choosing to cram into our days and nights? Is it a cultural addiction?

Latin American writer Isabel Allende, reflecting on her life in the NPR collection of faith essays *This I Believe*, begins with these words: "I have lived with passion and in a hurry, trying to accomplish too many things."[6] When I read those words, my first thought was to tear out the page and tape it to my bathroom mirror. It is a prayer of confession that cuts to the heart of my own life's imbalances.

There is an economic component to this for many of us. With stagnant wages in many fields, people feel compelled to work more hours per household than at any other time we can remem-

---

6. Jay Allison and Dan Gediman, eds., *This I Believe: The Personal Philosophies of Remarkable Men and Women* (New York: Henry Holt, 2006), 13.

ber. With job security tenuous in many industries, some people allow the lion's share of their vacation time to go unused, for fear the company will discover it can go on without them.

For others, the hyperactivity is rooted in unprecedented affluence. Some of us can afford to go places and to squeeze in experiences that once we could not afford financially. When you work sixty hours a week and spend another twelve on the road commuting, but then have money to spend, it seems a shame to miss the quick weekend trip to golf in the Bahamas or a friend's wedding in California. So we pack it all in.

In the big cities, where hundreds of thousands of cross-country professionals regularly intermingle, we occasionally fall in love with people who do not live in our neighborhood. Or even in our state. Quite a number of single professionals in my city are dating people who live 3,000 miles away on the West Coast. I did that myself briefly. This means that I squeezed in three extra cross-country trips in three months—paid for mostly with frequent flyer miles accrued from the travel that comes with making my living. I mastered the art of relaxing enough to get a decent sleep on a "red eye" flight back from the West Coast. I love the "red eye" for its efficiency in helping me accomplish something (such as travel across a continent) even when I am snoozing. When I can't sleep on a six-hour flight, I can knock off quite a bit of writing. "Multitask" is one of the more recent verb additions to the English language. It seems as American as apple pie to me.

For still others, our frenetic overfunctioning is based in loneliness or emptiness. Many of the evening activities, clubs, and organizations that adults join are primarily for human fellowship or for filling existential emptiness with something noisy. It's a bit like three-year-olds trying to keep themselves awake at ten o'clock at night.

For these and other reasons, many families have given up eating meals together or enjoying downtime on the back porch. Almost no one under the age of sixty watches the evening news

---

MINISTRY CLUE

In a busy culture, many participants will only manage to attend weekly events half the time or less. This should not necessarily be taken as a sign that they value their faith less than those who attend weekly. Sometimes work and complex life commitments just make weekly participation impossible. Consider:

- Developing phone shepherds who call all absentees for all events every week as a way of keeping in touch with people on the weeks when they are away. It is important that this contact be positive ("Hi, I am calling to check in on how you are doing this week. How can we be praying for you?") as opposed to nagging or negative ("We missed you on Sunday.")

- Taping missed services and sessions and automatically e-mailing these to people who were away.

■ ■ ■

---

anymore. A rapidly diminishing number of folks drink coffee over a newspaper in the morning. No time! Neighbors typically do not know one another well, especially in communities where transience is high and people do not perceive social investments in community building to be worth the trouble when they are expecting to relocate in just a few more months anyway.

And of course it should be no surprise that people who don't know how to sit still have difficulty sitting still for an hour in church or teaching their children to entertain themselves at home on a Saturday with scissors, paper, and a little imagination.

There are good reasons why most young adults choose to be anywhere but in church on Sunday mornings. However, one key factor is that Saturday night is now the party that functions as the Ultimate Reward for good boy scouts and girl scouts who labor all week long. I ask twenty-somethings with seventy-thousand-dollar jobs, "What time do you go to bed on Saturday night?" The common answer is around 2 A.M. Sometimes 3. Sometimes 4. When people go to bed that late (and often intoxicated), they probably won't be emerging back into the daylight before 10 the next morning—and when they do, they will move carefully first to their coffee pot, then to their running shoes, their *Washington Post*, their dog leash, their laundry basket, their corner café, and, maybe by noon, to their farmer's market. Then they begin to regroup and ready themselves for a new round of work on Monday—sometimes beginning with homework Sunday afternoon if the Redskins are not playing.

After the marathon intensity of the work week, the ritual of Saturday night–Sunday morning down time is a holy habit for millions of American workers. This is why many churches now offer major worship opportunities at times other than Sunday morning. Sunday night, Monday night, or Wednesday night each may be somewhat problematic times, falling on the tail end of the work day when people may be exhausted, but, compared to Sunday morning, these times may look good to people. In Washington, we helped to launch a downtown worship community on Wednesday evenings at 6:30 P.M. I heard people say that they give up their gym timeslot to share in a different kind of exercise. It fits into the rhythm of their week.

If I am going to offer Sunday morning worship that engages young adults, then I do not want to list a start time before 11 A.M., and 11:30 may even be better. However, once people have children, the kids may have everyone out of bed eating waffles by 7:30 in the morning, in which case a 9:30 or 10 A.M. worship time will make more sense.

Most people today are unwilling to give time for any experience they do not enjoy. Even the gyms pile up lots of largely unused memberships. Knowing we need it is one thing. Having a good time at it is quite another. But if it's meaningful *and* reasonably enjoyable, the folks in our downtown D.C. focus groups told

MINISTRY CLUE

Think short term:

- Four to six week study groups.

- One-time mission work projects that last two to four hours.

- If you encourage people to spend time both learning and serving, then set forth goals for a year, for example, to participate in three short-term studies and three mission projects as an alternative to participation in an ongoing study and an ongoing ministry team.

■   ■   ■

us, then it's worth ninety minutes of their time, maybe two hours. This is not adequate time for worship and a study group. It is enough time, however, for a sixty-five-minute worship experience and leisurely coffee interaction afterwards. You can add about fifteen minutes in the Latino and African American context, but even in these communities, younger adults tend to lack enthusiasm for the three-hour church services of their childhood. Ninety minutes is more than plenty.

Among young evangelical leaders, *Simple Church* by Thom Rainer and Eric Geiger has been one of the more talked-about books the last couple years.[7] The basic idea with a "simple church" is that it focuses on the most basic ingredients of Christian community—corporate worship, spiritual development, and serving others. Anything else is something for which few people have time. Furthermore, even of the three key areas just listed, many busy people will only make time for one or two. Most of the committee work, fund-raising schemes, policy meetings, building obsession, and ice cream socials that busy up mainline Protestant church life

7. Thom Rainer and Eric Geiger, *Simple Church: Returning to God's Process for Making Disciples* (Nashville: Broadman & Holman, 2006).

are accomplishing absolutely none of the core functions of a New Testament church. We should not be surprised that people have less and less time to offer for this spiritually peripheral stuff.

In a hyper-busy world, I need some things that the church is richly suited to offer me. Please spend your time with me carefully! Focus that time first and foremost on those activities that are most critical to my spiritual formation. Encourage me to take one or two nights during the week to spend time with my family. Teach me how to be still. And please try to offer at least one worship opportunity at a time other than Sunday morning, so that if I am a Sunday worker or a Saturday partier, I can still have a fair shot at sharing in the life of a vibrant faith community.

5

We Are Desperate for Authentic Community

In one of my earliest conversations with young adults in the D.C. area, a woman related a story of one of her friends who found herself new to the city and very isolated socially. This friend developed an attack of appendicitis, but she knew no one who could take her to the doctor or hospital. Her boyfriend and her parents were in other cities. So she called a taxi to carry her to the emergency room of the hospital, where she faced surgery all alone. As I visit with groups in my city, I tell that story and always heads nod.

One evening soon after that, I developed abdominal pains while I was sitting in an airplane about to fly to teach a pastors' seminar. I got off the plane. I changed my ticket to the following day and went home to sleep it off. By the early hours, I found myself riding a taxi to George Washington University Medical Center with what I thought was appendicitis but turned out to be kidney stones. I have rarely felt as alone as I did that night. This is what it's like to live as a single person, new to a large city. There are millions of Americans who can relate to this.

Finding friends, even casual friends, is an important task in the first months that we live in a new place. Finding people who

---

MINISTRY CLUE

Count how many small groups with between six and twenty people are currently functioning in the life of your church. Count only groups that meet at least twice a month.

Then divide your average worship attendance by the number of these groups. *(If some of the groups are essentially the same people wearing different hats, do not count them as a separate group.)* If you have a worship attendance of one hundred and you have six of this kind of group, then you have a ratio of one group to fourteen worshipers (1:14). I recommend that you shoot for one small group for every ten worshipers. In the case of a church of one hundred worshipers with six groups, the immediate task would be to create four new groups in the next year.

How many new groups does your church need?

■   ■   ■

---

call us by name, people we can go to when we need a cup of flour or an egg, people we can invite over for dinner occasionally or go with to a movie or ballgame—this is the kind of community many of us seek early in our residency in a new community. Finding this kind of community can be tricky, especially for single adults.

In May of 2008, a professional from the Gallup Organization worked with my church to facilitate two focus groups of downtown workers and residents in Washington. There were several astonishing discoveries that came from these conversation sessions. Among these:

- When a person or family moves to a new city, there is a natural progression of front-burner items to be addressed—roughly in this order: (1) a job; (2) a place to live; (3) issues of establishing residency—ranging from driver's license to locating the nearest dry cleaner; (4) finding friends. Finding a worship community was seen as a second-year priority, and then only if it appeared "we would be settling in the area for an extended time."

- Even people with positive past church experience seldom think of finding a church as a key part of establishing residency, nor do they think of a church as a good first place to develop new friends.

- People are far more likely to look for friends either online, at a bar, after hours at work, at the gym, at the dog park, or via hobby groups (running clubs, yoga classes, alumni clubs, and the like) than to look for friends at church.

- Even in cases where the churches are actually reaching lots of younger people, younger folks in the community may often still assume that there are mostly old folks behind the stained glass, and thus assume that there are few people *like them* in the church.

One of our conclusions from the focus groups is that the church needs to think of itself as being in the community-building business, and, in highly transient communities, the church must become and sell itself as *a place that helps people quickly discover a sense of home in a new city.* If we see ourselves only as a worship service, a lot of people who are open to our faith will procrastinate for months about checking us out—and possibly become so busy with other matters that there will be little time left for church.

Of course, human beings vary widely in terms of what feels to them like authentic community. Some churches invite people to shake hands during their worship time, resulting in a barrage of five-second encounters with strangers and remote acquaintances. I know many people who greatly enjoy such chit-chat, feeling that it demonstrates the friendliness of their church. Other people find such exercises useless and superficial. Likewise, even polite socializing around the coffee pot and the platter of cookies after worship is meaningful to some and shallow to others.

MINISTRY CLUE

Turbo groups are composed of eight to fifteen participants who meet for six to eight weeks, each of whom has been recruited as a potential future group leader. A turbo group may then create the leadership for six or seven new small groups within weeks of when the turbo group concludes. The first couple of weeks, the trainer(s) lead; then roles are intentionally passed around to group members, who each are responsible for segments of the group in the latter weeks.

In the latter phase of a turbo group, participants are led through a process where they decide what kind of group they would like to lead and whom they will ask to help them.

I recommend that these groups exist for a set period of time, somewhere between six and twelve weeks, and then conclude. People who have a good time will be back when new groups form. A church can run two to four generations of small groups in a year.

■   ■   ■

This is not a generational issue, so far as I can tell. I have watched persons of all ages enjoy light socializing. Most parties in the world are built on such casual, often frivolous interaction—and a lot of people enjoy parties. It is an essential matter of basic courtesy and hospitality to create a friendly, cordial environment in all church gatherings, and specifically to make intentional efforts to lead people to interact with those they do not know.

However, this level of community is not enough for any church!

Pay careful attention to this paragraph. Read it two or three times if necessary. In his book *The Search to Belong*, Joseph Myers talks about four types of social groups.[8] In each of these types of

---

8. Joseph R. Myers, *The Search to Belong: Rethinking Intimacy, Community, and Small Groups* (Grand Rapids, Mich.: Zondervan, 2003).

groups we feel connected and in community with others. Few churches excel at fostering all four types of belonging. (And this is okay.) I would modify Myers' four types of groups slightly to frame church groups as follows: In church life, I see (1) the mass event of more than 120 people, (2) the large social group/club of forty to 120 people, (3) the task-focused group of six to twenty people, and (4) the intimate group where you truly let your hair down. Any larger group, when examined carefully, may reveal several of the smaller types of groups within the whole.

Worship communities typically do well at the first two categories: the mass event and the large social group. I attended an NFL game last year where our home team creamed the Dallas Cowboys. At half time, I went to stand in a line for a hot dog. All around me total strangers were high-fiving one another; and then one stranger gave me a bear hug from behind, simply because I was wearing a Redskins hat and we were winning. Joy was in the air. Although we did not know one another at all, we discovered that day a common purpose and identity that was very meaningful to many. Have you been to churches like this? If people in your church are nervous about the church growing to a size where they cannot know everyone's name, your church is functioning as the second type of group. When groups exceed 120 in attendance, it is virtually impossible to know everyone's name. Breaking the 120 barrier in turn often allows the group to grow more easily in number. Most people in these largest types of communities move beyond an obsession with knowing everybody, and they are less likely to work to keep the group small enough so that they can know everybody.

In the first and largest type of group, I probably know some people by name, but most people simply as faces. In the second type of group I know people mostly as names that go with faces and little tidbits of information about them. In the third type of group (which might be a choir, a mission team, a study group, or a sports team) we begin to really learn the personalities of the various individuals and to get to know the significant life stories of some in the group. In the fourth, most intimate group, we find freedom to share honestly about aspects of ourselves that we would probably not advertise on our Facebook page. (You may invite only a handful of people into your fourth group in a lifetime.)

I believe that the third group is the key building block of church community. If we cannot move people beyond "passing the peace" and chit-chatting at the coffee pot into the third sort of group, our church will fail to establish long-lasting relationships with many of the people we seek to serve. Furthermore, these people will be left to look beyond the church to find the depth of community that they crave. (Please beware: though committees and administrative or institutionally focused groups may technically lie within the bounds of the third group, these are not the kinds of groups for which most people hunger. They desire groups that are more clearly relational and more directly related to spiritual development or to serving their neighbors.)

Some churches excel in the art of the third group (and multiplying such groups). If their worship communities are large enough to fall into the category of the first group (more than 120), these churches are uniquely positioned to grow and assimilate their neighbors into a faith community.

Leaders of small group ministries who make the fourth group the norm and goal of their church's community experience are often frustrated when most of their church's worshipers refuse to join such a group. The fact is that most people don't want to sit in someone else's living room and share intimately about their lives with six other people. (Even serving on the finance committee may sound better than that!) We are very discriminating in picking the people to whom we will bare our souls.

All over the world, churches that master the art of the third type of group offer a powerful sense of community to their members and constituents. If they learn how to grow new leaders and multiply such groups, these churches may grow very large and complex. In such rapidly growing churches, we may see mass wor-

---

MINISTRY CLUE

The types of small groups that your church can sponsor are as varied as your imagination! Just be sure that you are clear on components that will be common to all your groups:

- Prayer sometime during the group time

- Sharing and conversation around the topic and/or the prayer time. People enjoy being able to share what's on their mind.

- An activity that is part of the group's core identity (studying something, working on a mission project, playing a sport, singing, planning a church event)

- Focused conversation about inviting others to join and making a plan to do so effectively.

- Some kind of food/drink, even if it's very simple. Breaking bread together is a bonding activity with great biblical roots.

- Intentional hospitality where appropriate interest and welcome is extended to newcomers.

■　■　■

---

ship gatherings of more than a thousand people on one hand, alongside quite a few tiny groups of very intimate friends. The real building blocks of these churches are not the worship services, but the smaller groups. When the second or third types of groups are allowed to multiply within the larger church system, people can know the names of those alongside them in these smaller groups, so that knowing everyone in the worship experience is no longer so pressing a need.

Think about your church:

- Of the four types of groups I have listed here, which does your church do best?

- What are some examples of how your church has learned to create new groups alongside those that already exist?

- In what ways are you surprised that I consider the third type of group as the basic building block of church community as opposed to one of the other sizes? Why do you find this counterintuitive?

- If your church has less than 120 people in regular attendance (and most churches do), would you be open to growing to this level and beyond so that you would have a greater capacity to serve more of your neighbors?

Please remember that the people around your church are desperate for authentic community.

6

FAMILIES HAVE NEVER
COME IN MORE FLAVORS

THERE ARE MANY KINDS OF FAMILY. ANY CHURCH CAN PROVIDE safe space for various types of family and also offer ministry that helps strengthen the relationships in a family.

Forming new relationships and birthing new families are things we have done for millennia; and we human beings are not slowing down in our attempts to do this. For all that is changing in the world, our drive to form family with other human beings remains very strong. Yet long-term relationships and marriages are more difficult to sustain today than in times past, and parenting has become downright scary. What is your church doing to help people with these concerns?

In some communities the majority of households are two adults with at least one child in the house. The adults may or may not be married, or it may be a second marriage—but such households look very traditional. Many suburban churches customize their ministry for this type of family. There will continue to be millions of such families in America for years and years to come, in rural areas, suburban areas, and even deep in the middle of the city. People rearing children will continue to have a higher than

average rate of church affiliation. Regardless of the varied constituencies your church may serve, I urge you to keep an eye on
families with children at home, and to develop partnerships with
those families in helping them raise great kids.

As you do so, please be aware that there are increasing numbers
of families rearing children where both parents are of the same
gender. Furthermore, there are neighborhoods where the majority
of kids live with one of their parents, usually the mother, and where
the second most common family system is the mother and children
living with *her parents*: three generations in one house. All of these
families have similar aspirations for their children. Those of us in
the church can be excellent partners in offering a stable and loving
extended family to help children reach their potential.

In urban neighborhoods where the loft condos are going in,
we may discover that half or more of the households are comprised of one human being. In one D.C. neighborhood in which I
have worked, 70 percent of the population is made up of single
adults. In this case, the residential family unit may be a person and
her Siamese cat. She may think of her cat in ways that approach a
parent-child relationship. Is your church welcoming and affirming toward people who are single and who are not looking for a
partner? A significant number of persons have discovered that one
is a perfectly whole number. Some of them would be open to ro-
mance if it happened, but it is not something that they seek.

Is your church so focused on partnered people that you send
a signal to single people that they are abnormal? This could be
happening without your awareness. There is a very strong tradition within Christianity of singlehood as a holy, honorable, and
even superior life choice. Are single people highly visible in your
church's life? Are you balancing sermon illustrations and church
programming focus in such a way that it is just as relevant to single people as to partnered and married people?

This is not about political correctness. It is about hospitality and
relevance. One of the fastest growing types of households is the

---

MINISTRY CLUE

One of the ways that churches can bless families is to offer great premarital ministry, both in terms of couple counseling and also premarital couple retreats. If your church is welcoming toward the LGBT community, by all means, mix straight and gay couples in the premarital retreats! Most of the issues in long-term relationships are exactly the same regardless of sexual orientation. And this says to all who are seeking to form new families: you are welcome here, within the mainstream of our church life.

The same is true of a church's ministry with couples who are already together. Celebrating and helping people past their first, seventh, and twentieth anniversaries, helping them to strengthen their relationships with regard to those issues that are common as relationships mature—this is very relevant ministry to a community. It is possible for a church to offer a ministry to couples that reaches far beyond the bounds of its membership; in fact, you can become legendary on the community grapevine for excellence in this kind of ministry.

■　■　■

---

house full of multiple single people (or sometimes single and married) all sharing one big house. In the Christian context, these communities sometimes intersect with the New Monasticism movement, a movement of heightened life simplicity and communal orientation. The majority of homes with multiple singles living as one family unit are not monastic—simply economic. The members of such households do not sleep together; they are simply housemates, who relate to one another similarly to adult siblings. Over time, significant affection may develop among the fellow householders such that often these types of households are more intentional about common mealtime and organized chores than more traditional families. Couples without kids at home, of all ages—newly married, unmar-

ried, or married for thirty plus years—this is another rapidly growing group in America. More people are choosing not to have children. As we live longer, couples may spend more years in the phase
of life when their children are grown and moved away. These folks do
not have children motivating them out the door each Sunday morning to participate in a church. However, for such couples in their
midlife years, starting in the forties and extending into their sixties,
it is very common for at least one of the two persons to experience a
major renaissance of interest in spiritual exploration, practice, and
formation. Churches are dependable sources for helping midlife
couples to find other couples with whom to share friendship. In fact
they are much more dependable at doing this for midlife couples
than for young couples, since most churches tend to have fewer people under the age of forty than they have older than forty.

MINISTRY CLUE

Give a family issues survey, with anonymity preserved. Give
it to church participants and give it out in the community
also. Let people know that this most important part of their
lives is important to your church. You might include the following kinds of questions on your survey:

- List all the issues you can think of for couples in relationship
  and let people check where they would love to see their relationship stronger.

- Ask the same question but let people answer on behalf of their
  friends and kinfolk, according to their perception of their needs.

- List several kinds of ministries the church might offer to couples
  and families, as well as a blank for them to suggest other types
  of ministry: ask them to check any that they would attend.

- Have a ministry task group evaluate the data and help the
  church plan a couple of strong ministry responses.

■   ■   ■

And, of course, both couples and housemates are increasingly likely to come from different faith backgrounds. It is increasingly likely that a Jew and a Hindu might come together and form households, or a Christian and Buddhist, or a Pentecostal Christian and a Catholic Christian, and so forth. Multiple (and some would feel conflicting) religious icons may be sprinkled through the house. If children are a part of the home, they may experience rituals of initiation in multiple faiths. Multifaith families have been around for years, but they are clearly increasing rapidly now as a percentage of households. With good communication, respect, compromise, and willingness to find some sense of common spiritual journey, multifaith families sometimes are the healthiest households on the block. What kind of messages does your church send to these families in terms of affirming and welcoming them or perhaps hinting that they are less than the desired norm, since both adults may not join your church?

Look at the types of families in your church. List the various configurations you know of. Compare this to what your community's demographic report tells you about the occurrence of various family structures in the neighborhood. What kinds of families are probably going to mix most easily in your midst? Are you doing a good job of attracting and assimilating these kinds of families? What kinds of families may find it harder to fit in? Many people will feel more at ease in a church when they see others who are in a similar family situation. (A few people seem to be able to make themselves at home regardless of whether there are others like them in the church, but they are a decided minority.) How can your church help people see and connect with others who have similar life situations?

I am not suggesting that we honor every family situation as virtuous, or every marriage as worth preserving at all costs. When, for example, someone's spouse refuses to love her, sleep with her, or observe his vows of monogamy, that is a broken marriage. When abusive behavior becomes part of the family system, so that someone is left feeling like he or she lives in hell, that is a dysfunctional family. Any flavor of family that hurts and dishonors others needs

---

MINISTRY CLUE

One resource that your church might have to offer people who are seeking strong relationships is seasoned, healthy couples who can function as *mentors*.

When your church performs a wedding, how about pairing a new couple with an established couple in the church, so that they can build relationships with others who have navigated various life issues and learned a bit of the art of relationship?

When you want to offer a class or small group on relationship building, how about turning to a seasoned couple to lead the class or group?

It is good for long-term couples to serve as mentors—it gently forces these couples to tend to health in their own relationships, even as they seek to offer encouragement to others.

■　■　■

---

help. However, sometimes one person's misery in a relationship can be a wake-up call to the partner that something must give in order for the marriage to function well again. Sometimes the presence of children in a family motivates the adults to work hard at healing their relationship, so that their kids are honored and respected. Other times, the presence of children becomes an excuse for two adults to continue to stay together and to behave badly.

Where is your church in helping people sort through these questions? Does your community know that you are a resource to them in their family relationships? Does your church know that you are rooting for them?! How is your church helping your neighbors in the struggle to form and to nurture strong families? What do you want to do to help people? Might the answer to that question help you determine the focus for some of the small groups you will offer in days to come? How are you providing safe, welcoming space for multiple styles of family?

7

WE MAY BE RAISING A
GENERATION OF HEROES

THAT WE ARE PERHAPS RAISING A GENERATION OF HEROES MIGHT be news to some of you. When you see the teens descend on the mall near your home, *hero* may not be the first word that comes to mind. I would encourage you to look more closely at this intriguing generation that is growing up among us. Honestly, we don't know what the future holds. So many of the formative events, both globally and locally, that will shape this next generation into adulthood simply have not happened yet and cannot be predicted.

And yet we have some clues that the group coming up may have significant similarities to their great grandparents. Neil Howe and William Strauss are generational theorists. A few years back, in their book *Generations: The History of America's Future, 1584–2069*, they proposed the theory that powerful patterns of social mood and personality repeat roughly every four generations.[9] Generational theory is no absolute predictor of anything but it does offer some clues as to what the next two or three gen-

9. Neil Howe and William Strauss, *Generations: The History of America's Future, 1584–2069* (New York: William Morrow, 1992), 56.

erations might be like, how current generations will change with age, and how our progeny may differ from those of us who are reading this book.

My first awareness of generational theory came as a teenager, when I heard often about a so-called "generation gap." We were in the waning years of the Vietnam War, and the disconnect between the baby boomers, born 1946 to 1964, and their parents seemed (at the time) epic and unprecedented in human history. According to Howe and Strauss, the baby boomers were raised indulgently, resulting in a very narcissistic young adulthood (the Me generation), moving into a moralistic phase in their middle adult years (the rise of the Religious Right), and they will end their lives (perhaps ironically) as visionary leaders, similar in some ways to the leader generation who saw us through the Great Depression and the World War II.

Baby busters (Gen X people born 1965 to 1986) were a highly criticized generation as kids, emerging into young adults with a high sense of alienation. Based on past patterns, we can expect them to be pragmatists in their middle adulthood, and somewhat reclusive later in life. For the record: we do not anticipate the Gen X'ers to ever become a generation of widespread community builders or church builders. They tend to be anti-institutional. As a whole, they will live private lives.

Millennials (the people born 1987 to 2008) are different still. This is the generation for whom organized religion is largely meaningless if it is not engaged in direct mission, putting faith into action. All my colleagues who work in campus ministry echo this theme. These young people find tremendous meaning in giving. They are *not* a narcissistic generation as a whole, not even close. These young people, currently growing up all over America—some nearing college graduation, some still in kindergarten—grew up in an era when their parents were fearful of drugs and AIDS and violence. In some ways, they are being raised more protected than previous generations, in a world that *feels more dangerous* on many

---

MINISTRY CLUE

Great youth ministry is increasingly going to be a mix between serving others (especially persons who are poor or suffering) and playing together.

All teaching for millennial youth needs to be explicitly relevant to life challenges. It needs to engage them in conversation as they process the concepts. They have keen minds and can absorb all kinds of theological material, so long as it is directly connected to their life.

If you take teens on a mission trip or off to a camp setting, you create great opportunities for theological reflection on life and mission.

If you wish to begin a conversation with young people about creating a youth ministry, consider focusing the conversation around two poles: (1) What are the challenges of your life? (2) How do you want to change the world? Allow the studying and the serving opportunities to flow from there.

■   ■   ■

---

fronts.[10] Few people send their second graders out the door anymore on a solo one-mile walk to school. That was the norm when I (a late baby boomer) was in second grade. Times changed. We anticipate these protected ones with their fledgling civic impulses may be our next generation of heroes as young adults (paralleling the folks Tom Brokaw dubbed "the Greatest Generation"). What this will look like exactly, no one can tell. But if there is any substance beneath generational theory, the chances are good that people engaged in teaching, coaching, and mentoring children today are in fact mentoring some giants. By giants, I mean people who

---

10. Howe and Strauss, *Generations*.

will change the world, who will rally to a cause (or many causes) greater than themselves, just as a generation did in December 1941. I doubt that this new generation will almost unanimously rush off to fight a war—but we could well note that a significant and steady number of young men and women signed up for an almost certain ticket to Iraq or Afghanistan, even though these were not popular wars.

I am not convinced that the world is more dangerous today than it was forty years ago when we had a perilous nuclear arms race and much less media focus on domestic hazards ranging from automobile deaths to child molestation. But there is little doubt that this generation of parents feels more anxiety about protecting its children, especially from drugs and gangs.

The World War II generation came home in 1945, entered college in unprecedented numbers and proceeded to build modern America. The fifties were an age when a wave of new schools and churches came on line. Disneyland was built. IBM came of age. Great airlines and television networks arose (only to come on hard times within a quarter century). These people put Neil Armstrong and company on the moon.

Why am I telling you all this?

Because I want us to remember that there is not something unusually wrong with the young people that are coming up. They are not a different species from the older generation of folks who populate our churches. There may in fact be more wrong with tired church institutions that seem disconnected from their world than with the young people God has placed around us in community. A very remarkable and talented group of people is growing up among us. Yes, they get lost and in trouble, just like every other generation. They live with a somewhat different assortment of cultural challenges than their grandparents. They need to discover forgiveness and self-control and a whole array of virtues just like every other generation.

They need to meet Jesus. They really do. We owe them that.

But give them time, and a chance. In their own way, even with habits that may offend their elders, they may offer us our best shot in a long time to solve some world problems, to think about a world that is larger than ourselves, or perhaps to think even of their self-interest in ways that are wiser and more global.

Vast numbers of this new generation are growing up without any meaningful input or encouragement from the church. Others are utterly bored by a church that directs its energy far too inward when it could be giving itself to alleviating suffering and making a tangible difference in the world. If reaching their parents is not enough motivation to roll up our sleeves and seek to serve this generation of children and youth with a whole-hearted effort at relevant age-level ministries, then perhaps the awareness that both a young Ronald Reagan and a young Mother Teresa are riding a bicycle down our streets might yet inspire us to get more engaged. We would be wise to become allied with this group of young people. They are going places that the church needs to go. With the resources of our faith traditions, they will go even farther and the world will be the beneficiary.

And quite honestly, with respect to Ronald Reagan, I personally wish that the church had truly shared some more formative time with him. For all Reagan's good instincts and optimistic spirit lent to this country, there were some significant blind spots that kept both him and us as a nation from rising fully to the challenges that were before us in the 1980s.

Well, good news! We get another chance.

Look again at the kids running down the hall at your church and down the sidewalk in front of your church's building. Thank God for them! Pray for them, and give your best toward the task of cultivating spiritual giants.

8

WE HAVE MASTERED THE ART
OF COMPARTMENTALIZING

COMPARTMENTALIZING IS THE PRACTICE OF ACTING IN LIFE with disregard for the bigger picture. It is about disregarding how our actions may have consequences beyond what we can see or disregarding details about a person or a situation that we do not want to see. It is a human coping mechanism and probably has some value as a survival skill. Compartmentalizing is not new. However, the implications of this human tendency are unique in any era, including our own.

When high-ranking German Nazis managed a barbarous and murderous regime by day and then came home to bounce their blond children on their knees in the evening, there was some heavy-duty compartmentalizing going on. It is not difficult, from our vantage point, to see the fundamental inconsistency that ran like a deep fault through their lives.

Most compartmentalizing is less dramatic. We see it when people choose to vote for one political candidate whom they "like," when in fact they agree more with the positions of the other candidate. In order to make a positive identification with candidate A, they somehow block out messages from candidate A that they do not like or wish to hear. They compartmentalize, choosing to focus on aspects of their candidate that cause them to feel good. Savvy campaign propagandists quickly discern when this is going on in a voting population and exploit it in their advertising strategies.

You may decide to marry someone who would appear, to the dispassionate bystander, as a very odd choice of spouse for you. Perhaps the bystander can see that you constantly argue with your fiancé or that you two have life goals that are headed in opposite directions. You are just as capable of seeing these things, but you choose not to focus on them. In the passion of romantic love, people often choose to block out very obvious and important information about the person they are marrying. We compartmentalize.

In terms of religion, the capacity for compartmentalizing means that a lot of folks make decisions about participating in a certain church aside from certain very important factors. They may see in a certain church a particular personal benefit that overrides other concerns: a good environment for their kids, feel-good music, the presence of other people their age, a happy ambiance that offers a good escape from other aspects of their life, a very likeable pastor who remembers their name.

Whatever it is that draws us in to participate in a faith community, *it is very likely there will be aspects of that community that we do not like.* We choose to tolerate these other aspects of community life, or perhaps to tune them out altogether. We compartmentalize—because in certain ways the church *works* for us and for our family.

This may begin to explain why young liberal Europeans used to go gaga every time Pope John Paul II appeared in public. The man was a rock star with young adults in Europe, and to some degree in the United States. These same persons rarely connected that this beloved grandfatherly figure was dead set against birth control, divorce, premarital sex, gay rights, women as clergy, and military action of almost any kind. And yet people who differed with him on many of these issues still loved the man. His smile

---

MINISTRY CLUE

Talk to some of the people at your church. Ask the following questions:

- What is it that keeps drawing you back to our church week after week, year after year?
- What do you think draws in our newer members?
- What do you have to *put up with* in order to share in the life of this place?
- If you could add, change, or improve one thing that we do in order for us to be more inviting to your friends, what would it be?
- Would you tolerate that change? Would others?

■ ■ ■

---

gave them warm fuzzies. His ambiance made them feel good. They compartmentalized.

Have you ever wondered why quite a few high-powered, intelligent career women attend churches that stalwartly deny women equal rights with men? Is it odd to find such women not just attending *but taking notes* as a patriarchal pastor waxes lyrical, advancing a theological worldview that marginalizes and subjugates them? That's compartmentalization!

Here are a few hard truths about compartmentalizing that most moderate and left-of-center churches do not yet get:

- *A lot of people out there agree with us more than they agree with conservative evangelicals, but these people are probably not going to attend church anyway.* While there might be such a thing as a liberal base for political movements, that base is usually very tenuous for religious movements. For left-of-center folks, there is a more important issue than finding a place where people agree with them on various issues. More important is finding a place that is truly worth their time. Since most of these folks cannot imagine church being a good use of their time, our positions on various issues become largely irrelevant to them. By the tens of millions in America, they remove themselves from the market of potential church-goers. In so doing they inhibit the growth and relative influence of moderate and liberal churches.

- *If we remain open to the possibility of church participation, please note that we also possess the capacity for bracketing out that which offends us, in order to make the place "work" for us.* This is no different than picking and choosing what we will take from a salad bar, skipping beets and anchovies, for example. We may hate the beets, but we can still build a good salad at that bar. Sometimes, left-of-center folks who wish to practice faith in community will choose a more conservative church despite certain theological quirks, especially if a more conservative church has a vibrant sense of life about it, and a lot of people. It also works the other way: right-of-center people may choose a more liberal church, despite certain theological quirks, especially if the liberal church exudes a greater sense of grace and caring.

- *A LOT of people care little about theology or politics,* even if these issues may affect them more directly than they recognize. A church with a heavy "issue orientation" may bore them or turn them off entirely . . . even if they essentially agree with the positions. I do not encourage any church to diminish its convictions, but rather to be aware that there are legions out there who would consider being part of your church who will never be passionate one way or another about your theological nuances.

- *Of the people who are willing to explore participation in a faith community, most come to us first as consumers.* They may commit to the community's traditions and life eventually—but at first they are mostly spiritual shoppers. Woe to the church that fails to understand this! Most people are looking first for relevant, comfortable, and inspirational worship experiences that fill them with hope and good feelings. Many are looking for great children's ministries. Most are looking for down-to-earth people, including some who look like them. Most are looking for churches that reach out to those who suffer. Most are looking for simple coherent spiritual principles that can help create a sense of order and comfort in the chaos of their personal lives. Woe to the church whose motto is that there are no simple answers. I strongly urge any such church to think again about that.

Evangelicals typically are far more market-savvy than mainline Protestants. At times, however, they have won the crowd, but lost the cause—creating feel-good communities largely devoid of theological mindfulness or scholarly biblical literacy. Evangelical Sally Morganthaler's 1995 classic *Worship Evangelism* is one of the more thoughtful critiques of evangelical excess in watering down content for the sake of marketing.[11] We may be able to get people in the doors with various tactics and topics, but do we manage to take them somewhere? Do we offer them something more than they may have come looking for? Mainline Protestants also can water down content for the sake of marketing; but more often than not, mainline churches either do not market themselves at all or they fail to explore the complexity and the deepest *felt needs* within the people they desire to engage.

I said earlier in these pages that cheap consumerism is our enemy. We want to lead people beyond using church as cheap therapy or a place where they cherry-pick beliefs or experiences á la carte. We want to take them on a deeper spiritual journey that

11. Sally Morganthaler, *Worship Evangelism: Inviting Unbelievers into the Presence of God* (Grand Rapids, Mich.: Zondervan, 1995).

MINISTRY CLUE

It is important for churches to understand the concept of *felt needs*.

When my son was eight, I made him sit at the dinner table for two hours once in order for him to finish eating the eight green beans that had been placed on his plate. Green vegetables are a need that human beings have, but for eight-year-olds, they are usually not a felt need.

As a pastor, I do not have this kind of leverage over people. There may be all sorts of things that my church believes people need. But we will only engage people when we approach them first on the basis of what they think they need.

Addiction recovery groups, recreational opportunities, positive peer communities for preteens, seminars or services focused on strengthening relationships—these are all entry-level possibilities into a church's life that meet various needs. As churches speak to people's felt needs, they begin building relationships with the larger public—relationships that can eventually move much deeper into the full exploration of a faith tradition and practice.

■ ■ ■

---

includes learning and wrestling with key stories and practices within our faith tradition, a journey that stretches them and us beyond narcissistic materialism into a life of caring for others. But if we do not take the time to discover and observe their deepest motivations and perceived needs in coming to us, the majority of the people we could be reaching may end up in another church or remain on a solo journey spiritually. The church that connects with them may come with a very different worldview than they share— but it will almost certainly be a church that is paying very close attention to what church participants most deeply desire in life.

People can *and probably will* bracket out much of the rest.

We have mastered the art of compartmentalizing.

Part Two

THE ONLY THING CERTAIN IS THE JOURNEY

9

My Journey to the City

When I was eleven years old, I traveled to San Francisco for the very first time. My father was the keynote speaker for a convention at one of the downtown hotels. We lived in the Los Angeles suburbs, in a world very different from the bustle and verve of San Francisco. The energy of the city mesmerized me. After Dad's speech, he and I drove the coastal highway together back to southern California. In those curving, formative three hundred miles, we talked about all manner of topics for two days. We talked a lot about cities, including the long-standing reputation of the city among rural types as being the root of all that is evil. It was on that winding road home from San Francisco that I sensed a call to ministry for the first time. As that call unfolded in the coming years, I often dreamed of spending my life in a place like San Francisco, where it seemed as if every sort of human being and ideology was deposited on the same city block and asked to live in community.

A few years later, my family joined an inner-city church, where my father became the pastor. Granted it was a relatively small city, about a hundred thousand in population, but our church was located in a neighborhood that had undergone enormous social and economic change as a result of the confluence of new cultures,

MINISTRY CLUE

Have you or your church leaders ever taken a prayer walk in your city?

Prayer walks are a gift to us from the Pentecostal movement. There is something about walking and praying with eyes wide open that is immensely helpful, especially in cities.

You cannot know a city simply from driving forty-five mph down its streets. Prayer walking allows you to move at a slower pace and to really see and hear what is happening in a place, to take in details that you have likely missed before.

It helps to keep a journal to reflect on what you saw, and to walk with others who can (after the walk) reflect and compare observations and thoughts from the walk.

Before your church rushes off with a new ministry, take an afternoon to walk your mission field, even to stop and chat with a few folks, and to give God space and opportunity to show you some things you need to see.

■ ■ ■

poverty, and crime. While the church across the street from us chose to sell their building and move out to more suburban pastures, our church chose to stick it out and to thrive where we were planted. That church is still there thirty years later, on the corner of 18th and Bosque in Waco, Texas, stronger today than then. I loved that church. I loved that neighborhood.

However, for reasons that only God fully understands, every church that I would serve in ministry for the next quarter century was located either in a rural or suburban community. In 1993, I was recruited by a growing congregation in a Florida beach community, where I would serve on the pastoral staff for nine years. During those nine years, the membership of that church would double from two thousand to four thousand. We saw hundreds of adults join that church by profession of faith. The heart of thriving Protestant ministry in America at the end of the twentieth century was NOT in the city, but in the suburbs.

In 2002, I left my position at the Florida church to begin coaching churches and pastors and to oversee various new church development efforts. During the next five years, I worked with a couple of hundred churches in a variety of denominations and settings, ranging from inner city to open country, from the secular terrain of twenty-first-century Toronto, Ontario, to the decidedly church-friendly terrain of Dothan, Alabama. I worked with new church development projects on the plains of west Texas, in the Cascade foothills of Oregon, in the rustbelt of Ohio, in a historic community in Virginia, in the remote regions of Michigan's Upper Peninsula, and in every sort of neighborhood from Mobile, Alabama, eastward along the northwest Florida coast, from inner city neighborhoods to open country. The new churches did not all take root. Some fared better than any of us could have imagined. A couple may become megachurches. Getting to work with visionary, creative, and courageous Christian leaders in such a variety of contexts has been one of the greatest blessings of my life.

Before very long, I was feeling a strong inner tug to get off the sidelines of coaching and to spend some time on the ministry front lines in a very different context. I decided that I was finally going to find my way deep into the city, in response to what by now felt like an almost primal sense of calling, to develop faith community in an urban context. I began to look around the United States and to converse with friends in such cities as Chicago, Indianapolis, Cincinnati, Tampa, and Washington, D.C. In each city, I found old neighborhoods in various stages of redevelopment, with a sense of burgeoning energy and possibility where almost all hope had been lost a few years earlier. The churches struggled to keep up with the constant demographic changes. Many churches had closed or moved to the suburbs. Others carried on with only a remnant of the numbers of people they once served. Parishes that once numbered thousands of members might have fifty left. One denomina-

MINISTRY CLUE

The easiest people in the cities to herd together into church communities are new residents of ethnic enclaves, many of whom are Christian immigrants, married and raising kids in a new land. For these folks, church becomes the cultural and community center for their families during their first generation in America, and beyond. Most historic congregations miss out on the opportunity to provide a base for such ethnic faith communities. A few churches seize upon this opportunity and help to serve hundreds of people who would never otherwise wander into their Euro-American 11 A.M. worship service.

If your church is located in a community with new immigrant populations, why not consider sponsoring or partnering with a new congregation that serves one or more of these groups? This is more than simply renting space. This is shared ministry and a proven road to revitalized ministry for many urban churches.

■ ■ ■

tional leader, as he toured me around his city, remarked that most of the established churches were at least "two major demographic shifts behind" in terms of keeping up with the changes in their community. (For example, the working class Euro-Americans may have moved out in the 1960s, followed by an influx of African American working class, who are now largely displaced by a Hispanic immigrant community. A surviving church may find itself ministering primarily to a group of aging folks who have not lived in the central city for forty years, or it may have changed gears entirely, so that the current membership bears little connection to the church's Eurocentric past.)

Most of the new churches in the center of our large cities are conservative evangelical or fundamentalist in theology. (Notable exceptions include the Metropolitan Community churches and a few of the African American megachurches.) A significant number of city dwellers are unable to relate to any of the major options for church involvement in their communities, due to issues of language, culture, sexual orientation, musical taste, or political perspective. Even pros at compartmentalizing cannot always close their eyes to that which is downright offensive. The college-educated professionals who are repopulating our central cities are often more difficult to herd than suburbanites. That a person is prone to question what he or she encounters often correlates with a distrust of institutional expressions of religion.

In the urban context, the new homeowners buying the gentri-fied housing and loft condos are more likely than before to be single, childless, gay, highly educated, raised in a non-Christian home, or transient (due to a job with government or industry that keeps them regularly moving all over the nation or the planet). With each of these factors that we add to an individual's personal profile, we lower the chances, statistically, that this person will be involved with organized religion.

In the summer of 2007, I moved to the ninth largest urban area in America to partner with a handful of established churches in the city to create new opportunities for faith community. Despite considerable acumen in reading demographic reports, I actually had no clue what I was getting into. Washington, D.C., would prove to be unlike any other place I had ever known. The plan was experimental from the outset; no mainline church had a direct precedent for what we were attempting. All the models were based in different circumstances, either demographically or theo-logically. Without precedents, there was little way to define what our chances were in achieving our vision.

I cannot overstate what a year of surprises awaited me. From a three-bedroom Florida house with big trees and a white picket fence I moved to downtown Washington and a small tenth-floor condo overlooking Massachusetts Avenue between the White House and the U.S. Capitol. From the first day, the work was difficult and the community largely nonresponsive. The lack of response will go down as one of the great surprises of my life. It never occurred to me that God would call me to a project and then it not flourish. In the strange months ahead, I would begin to wonder if perhaps God's greater purpose in this exercise was to teach me some important things about the world that is coming.

D.C. is an especially tricky city for church development. In the condos that snake along the Metro lines, there is probably a higher per capita collection of graduate degrees than any other city in America, and a more varied collection of national origins than almost anywhere else on earth. D.C.'s young elite are a reflection of several realities: first, an array of idealists who come to work for the nonprofits and lobbying firms; next, a mix of true believers and opportunists who cozy up to whatever presidential administration is in power; next, career-builders working their way loyally up the ladder in various federal agencies and law firms; and, finally, *the best of the best* from top universities around the world who are in town simply to pad their resumes as interns, consultants, or grad students in preparation for lives of influence and power. They work ridiculous hours, striving to make their mark, to excel so as to be noticed.

Then after a six-day work binge, the bars of Adams Morgan overflow on Saturday night, with a mass of young pedestrians so thick by 2 A.M. on Sunday that some streets become like parking lots, with traffic virtually frozen. By 10 A.M. the same morning, most of the people I came to D.C. seeking to reach are either sound asleep, hung over, or enjoying the one morning of the week when they can take a long run, play with the dog, or read an actual paper copy of the complete *Washington Post*. Most of these people are not going to be attending any Sunday morning worship service anywhere anytime soon.

There are apartment buildings in our city core where the majority of residents turn over in less than a year. Best estimates place the percentage of unchurched residents in the neighborhoods we work at greater than 80 percent. (I should note there is a higher rate of church affiliation in D.C.'s historic black neighborhoods and out in the suburbs where the population turnover is a bit slower and in any neighborhood where families are raising children.)

Finally, like many cities, D.C. is a place of extreme economic contrasts. The haves and the have-nots are often next-door neighbors. The neighborhood where I live is loaded with the upwardly mobile fast and trendy set I have just described, paying outrageous prices for tiny condos with close access to Metro stations and hip restaurants. Yet, hardly a mile away, we have rats in the streets, running between dilapidated apartment buildings and crack houses. And all about us, we have several thousand folks, mostly lifetime residents of our city, who live on the street or in shelters.

My experience stepping into this city turned out to be as much an adventure in my own spiritual formation as it was an adventure in renewing the witness of historic urban churches. I developed partnerships with churches in four mainline denominations, and we created ministries in three sites, involving dozens of people. However, it became clear very quickly that our ministry plan was too expensive given the slow growth prognosis. In particular, we brought suburban salary structures into a setting that proved itself unlikely to underwrite such costs. As I write this book, some of our initiatives are thriving and others are struggling. I asked God for an adventure and, oh my goodness, I got one!

Yet every day we learn something.

One of the most important things I have learned personally is that, despite the enormous challenges in my first attempt at this sort of ministry, I am more in love with the city than ever: the diverse people, the energy, the architecture, the sporting events, the arts, the constant process of rebirth. Even the pain and suffering of the city around me engage my mind and heart.

More important still, *I learned anew that the journey of faithfulness is the one thing we know for sure.* In good seasons, and in lean, that journey continues. Our calling continues. For two decades, I served in contexts where we posted net gains in all the key people measures year after year. Increasingly, as a coach and consultant, I work with churches in challenging territories where they have not seen net gains in many years. I work with pastors who, though they may refuse to lead a dying church, labor in the trenches where the gains are very slow. They and their churches may reframe their ministry in terms of focusing on what is living—and yet the progress is not always apparent, and discouragement is always but a moment away.

The pages ahead move us beyond a focus on our changing ministry context to consider now *our journey* as persons and churches who seek to be faithful and relevant in whatever context we find ourselves in. Your church may soon figure out a way to break through and connect with larger numbers of your neighbors—or you may already have found that way. I think it is important that we keep trying to do just that. Sometimes it takes years of prayer. *You still matter to God and your church still matters to God, even in the night season when you can't quite see what to do to advance your church's mission and ministry.* Even in puzzling times, our journey with God and *our relationship with God* go forward.

My journey has carried me a long ways from where I began. Where is your journey carrying you? Where is God leading?

10

GETTING UNSETTLED

PILGRIMS AND *SETTLERS* ARE OPPOSITES. PILGRIMS MAY STOP traveling at some point and decide to settle down—but when they do this, they cease to be pilgrims. Settled people and settled, established, routine-minded churches may not feel a thrill when offered the invitation to pull up stakes and go on a journey with God.

The publisher of this book is an outfit called The Pilgrim Press. It is a publishing arm of the United Church of Christ, a denomination with diverse roots, some of which go all the way back to the folks who came to New England on the Mayflower in the early years of European immigration to the New World. However, the majority of UCC congregations today (as with all mainline denominations) are settled people, and slowly shrinking in size. When I take growing UCC churches as a subset within the larger denomination, the difference between them and their denomination as a whole is clear: the growing churches tend to be pilgrim churches, intentionally on the move, *striving* to reach new populations, to try new ministry strategies, and to frame the Christian good news in fresh categories and metaphors.

I am working right now as consultant to the pastors of a certain pilgrim New England congregation that chose to sell its building and move into rented space for a time while they search for a facility more appropriate to their life and activities. They did not abandon their neighborhood, just their building. They had been settled in that building a long time. They almost died in that cavernous place. The chances of their rebirth greatly increased when they made the audacious decision to become pilgrims again. They tapped into a biblical theme as old as Abraham, reiterated again in the story of Jesus calling disciples—a theme of leaving the settled place to go on a journey with God. Churches do not have to sell buildings in order to become adventurers again—but selling an aging and oversized building rarely hurts them.

It has long been recognized that growth rates of new churches slow down after a few years, after deep relationships form and a comfortable house of worship begins to feel like home. Many churches eventually get so settled and comfortable that they forget about the world outside their doors almost entirely, except as a venue for token acts of mercy and the collection of special offerings. About ten years after a congregation is planted, we often see a significant slowdown in its growth.

Why, then, do we see congregations that have been around for several generations suddenly deciding to become unsettled and to take risks, to embark anew on an adventure with God that will carry them into an unknown place? Why do they embark without any assurance that their journey will save their church as an institution? I observe different reasons in different places.

Desperation. When a church sees the money running out, or finally feels incapable of affording the facility repairs, or many of the leaders simultaneously feel tired of the burden of carrying the church on their shoulders, then it may reach the point of desperation. Such a church is moving very close to the end of its life. In the months (or possibly few years) between the point where the leaders collectively see the handwriting on the wall and "the End," there is a window of opportunity. In this window, we may be desperate enough to try things or to allow others to try things that we would clearly not have tried five years ago. When bold decisions are made, sometimes the desperate church will lose half its members in protest. Some of these folks who leave may have been looking for an excuse to do so for some time. If the remaining remnant hangs together, trusting God, amazing things often happen. I love working with such churches because usually they are willing to do whatever it takes; they have become pilgrim people once again.

Crisis. Sometimes a different kind of crisis arises, the kind that does not threaten to close the church or provoke feelings of desperation, but still throws the church into a spin. It may be an economic issue, where a plant closes and a third of the church's budget dollars suddenly dry up. It may be a community or national tragedy that upsets the settled homeostasis around town and opens up a raw sense of our profound need for God. In the community I served in Florida, our church experienced growth spurts after both the September 11, 2001, tragedy and also after an epic hurricane. In such times, we may be laying off staff and simultaneously expanding ministry—and the chaos demands finding new ways to get the work done. (Sometimes this is the oppor-

---

MINISTRY CLUE

Is your church facing a crisis of some sort? Many churches are. Even if the crisis is not of a degree to provoke widespread desperation, it could be a great opportunity for getting your church out of a rut.

Have your leaders stepped back to consider how the crisis you face can be leveraged as an opportunity to change the way you function as a church?

Start that conversation quietly, one-by-one and two-by-two. Don't take that conversation into an official church meeting until some great "Aha's" start to bubble up on the sidelines.

■　■　■

tunity to gracefully end a staff relationship that has gone on five or ten years too long, freeing up valuable resources for better use.)

Rising up of a visionary. Someone has a bright idea. Someone sees a new possibility. Vision typically comes first to individuals. Occasionally, two people may see it simultaneously and apart from each other. The visionary person could be a pastor. It could just as likely be a person in the church who has been praying about the church's future. The visionary person says to the rest of the group, "Wait a second. It doesn't have to be like this. It could be this way instead. Stop, look, think about it. Can you not see it as well?" If the visionary person has the people skills to convince others to consider this new possibility, then a visionary community is born within that church. If this visionary community begins praying together and studying the book of Acts, watch out! I will reiterate that the visionary person does not have to be the pastor. But if the pastor is resistant to any vision taking hold in the congregation, there may be conflict or a change of pastors in the offing. No matter where the vision starts in a congregation, part of a pastor's role is to converse actively with the church's vision and to serve as a primary advocate.

An infusion of new people. Sometimes the neighborhood changes yet again and a new group of people begins to populate the church, bringing a new sense of energy and life. Or one dynamic family joins the church, and twenty others follow them in the next six months: their extended family and/or their friends. Many central city churches have been transformed by the arrival of church-going gay and lesbian folks buying the fixer-uppers in the neighborhood. I served a rural church once that was saved by two amazing families who united with us within a few months of each other, transforming that place and suddenly enlarging our sense of God possibilities. That church had been simply an open-country chapel, with almost no energy for anything except the annual homecoming/cemetery day. Yet with the infusion of new folks, they suddenly had the energy to build a children's Sunday school annex in a single weekend. Although the church had been settled there for over a century, the people suddenly became pilgrims again.

A part of our ministry plan in Washington has been to help infuse new people into historic churches by developing new worship communities alongside longstanding communities, even meeting in the same worship space at different hours, with an interplay of people from the old and new churches coming together in ministry and mission. I must say, however, that the best partners for us were already *decidedly pilgrim* in their orientation toward God's future for their church before we came along. We didn't make pilgrims out of them.

Spontaneous combustion. If I were a bumper sticker kind of guy, I would consider a bumper sticker that reads, "Pentecost happens." It happens in all kinds of seasons. It can happen at any point in a

---

MINISTRY CLUE

Don't forget Jim Collins' brilliant lesson from *Built to Last: Successful Habits of Visionary Companies* (New York: Harper-Business, 1994), 43, "to avoid the tyranny of the OR." It may be possible for your church to venture out in a journey with God while retaining a comfort zone, a settled zone for those among you who deeply value familiar routine. Sometimes (but not always) it is possible to retain ministries that continue virtually unchanged even as enormous changes are occurring all around the church.

When we say to these members that we will seek to keep a comfort zone for them in the midst of change, we are saying, "We love you, and we value your place in our community of faith." They in turn may become cheerleaders for innovative ministry once they see that it does not threaten what they cherish and wish to preserve.

■   ■   ■

---

church's life cycle. It often happens when a group of people is in a praying or spiritually open mode. If several persons in the church are going through a season of personal spiritual renaissance, this also helps. Spontaneous combustion is when the Spirit of God simply lights a fire under a group of people, often after a very slow, settled season.

Settlers within churches may view any of these events I've been describing as threatening. There is nothing morally wrong with settlers—they are often hard workers and loyal friends—but anything that promises to unsettle their church or community scares them. I have watched the most graceful people seem to change personalities when something threatened the settled nature of their church life. Once I met with a church that was thinking about leaving its building and meeting temporarily in the convention facility of the local Holiday Inn. I will never forget a young woman with two children and a husband in tow, who stood up in our meeting to announce with great drama and a quiver in her voice, "When these girls were born I made a vow unto God I would take them to church, and I do not intend to take them each Sunday to a motel." With that, her household paraded out the center aisle and through the back door never to be seen again. It shocked several in attendance. They knew that woman as a cheerful, can-do kind of person, quick to volunteer and help out in all sorts of ways. But she was a settler, and her church was becoming unsettled.

Please resist the temptation to demonize the people who are not happy about the prospect of your church becoming a pilgrim people. Be kind to them. Hold your tongue. Pray for them. But, on the other hand, when people make grand exits from committees or from the church itself, DO NOT (I repeat DO NOT) chase them into the parking lot begging them to reconsider. If your church can't let some settlers go, you will probably never get very far on the journey God has for you.

Funny as it may sound, relationships with God have always been unsettling to people.

11

WHO SAID IT WOULD BE EASY?

THE FIRST-CENTURY CHURCH EXPANDED IN PART BECAUSE OF A convergence of several factors that made expansion possible—good roads, political stability, Jewish settlement throughout the Roman Empire, and so on. The first century was a ripe and unprecedented moment in world history for the spread of a faith such as Christianity. But the New Testament record indicates that even in favorable circumstances for church development, the way of the apostles was hard. Authentic ministry is always hard. Speaking truth to power, advancing values that may not be accepted by the wider culture—these things are hard to do.

When Paul the Apostle arrived in the Greek city of Philippi some time around 50 C.E., we are told in the book of Acts that he healed a slave girl possessed by a demon that enabled her to tell fortunes. Paul quickly ended up as a defendant in court, in a case pressed by the girl's owner, who claimed that Paul's benevolence had in fact ruined his business. Paul went to jail for that. This was the jail in which he and Silas famously sang hymns at midnight followed by the earthquake.

It wasn't the only time that Paul ended up in big trouble as he sought to plant new Christian cells in various cities across the Roman Empire. About one fourth of the New Testament is comprised of authentic and symbolic correspondence between Paul and the spiritual pioneers he left to continue Christian ministry in these Roman cities. These letters are, in part, therapeutic journaling by the first missionary pastor, working through how hard his work was, and how painful.

The work of the spiritual pioneer is hard. The work of the missionary is usually painful. The work of the prophet is often deadly. There is no way around it. Anyone who thinks that a project will be easy simply because God is in it has not accounted for the biblical model. From Moses to Elijah to Jesus to the apostles—their work was ridiculously difficult. Why should it be different for us today?

Christian ministry is rarely ever a cakewalk. Even in very established ministry settings where the churches are highly influential and respected, even when the pastors of such churches are gifted, faithful, and sensitive to others, such pastors may find themselves in painful conflict with church members who are personally wounded or fearful of change.

In August of 2006, I spent four days wandering around Washington and Arlington, just studying the city, watching people, noting the patterns of new residential development, and listening for what God had to say to me about it all. At this point, I had not yet agreed to come to work here; it was simply a season of spiritual exploration. The energy of the rebuilding throughout the central city was electric! Cranes dotted the urban horizon in every direction. And yet, by the end of my four-day tour, there was one thought that lodged in my brain: "Developing a new faith community here will be very hard work—especially as an outsider to the city. It is one of the hardest possible ministry tasks I could ever consider. It is probably so difficult as to be unadvisable."

And then a very strange thing occurred.

I was thinking about the difficulty of the ministry task in D.C. as I rode down the long escalator during Friday evening rush hour into the Dupont Circle Metro Station. In the midst of wall-to-wall people deep in the earth waiting for the train, I noticed a woman with her dog. She was blind. She was quadriplegic, with slight use of her hands, enough to move her fingers across a Braille magazine as she waited for the train. She was dressed in a business suit, apparently traveling home from work. Her guide dog rested in front of her wheelchair. I marveled at the courage of this woman, who had surely practiced with her dog many times moving from home to work and back again, by faith.

The train arrived, and I moved onboard with the hordes of people. I looked back to see: and sure enough, the dog entered the Metro car, followed by the woman in the wheelchair. At the next stop more people crowded onto our car, obscuring her from my sight. When, at the following stop, several people got off the train, I looked again and she was no longer there. Had the alternate door opened? I don't think so. I puzzled for a moment about where she could have gone; then my mind traveled elsewhere.

Later that evening, when it was time for bed, I reflected on my day and on whether or not to accept an invitation to come to this city to develop a network of new faith communities. I wished aloud that I could just have a vision of Jesus in my sleep telling me what to do. How easy that would be.

I awakened around 2 in the morning, and the first thought that came to me was that Jesus had not made an appearance in my dreams during the night. I rolled over to go back to sleep. And then with my mind's eye, I saw her again as clearly as the first time, reading her Braille magazine, carefully and courageously navigating a frenzied and complicated world she could not see, trusting her life to a dog. I had asked for a vision of Jesus that night. And in God's way, I got one.

My apprehension about the task of working in this city was simply that it would be hard. That was my concern, my complaint. But then I saw the woman on the Metro, a Christ figure with challenges far more intense than mine would be, bearing witness that we must be faithful in that which we are called to do. She did what

MINISTRY CLUE

Are you and/or your church assuming that your work should be easy? Where do such assumptions come from?

Sometimes such assumptions come from an overidealized memory of our church's past. Compared to the challenges of today, the 1960s or '70s may look easy in retrospect.

But those were not altogether easy times. Sometimes the most helpful things to remember about our church's past are the difficulties we navigated. Please forget about the beloved pastor who had the good fortune of serving your church during your supposed heyday. Perhaps that person had the right set of gifts for that moment in time— but he or she would likely be the wrong pastor for your church in the new millennium that you face.

The most important legacy that your church has is its history of navigating difficulties in times past, not the aspects of its ministry that may have come easier then.

When has your church shown courage? When did it beat the odds? When did it act like Jesus on the Metro, determined to do what it had to do? Therein lies a clue to the church you need to be today.

■ ■ ■

life required her to do, no matter how hard. If cultivating new faith communities in Washington was the right thing for me to do, the difficulty of the task was irrelevant.

Granted, I am always looking for the easiest way to accomplish any task. But, then, the Great Commission does not come with a promise of being easy. Rather, it comes with the promise that God will be with us in the doing.

The work of my predecessors—of Jesus, of the first-century apostles and even the nineteenth-century American frontier evangelists—was hard work. My direct ancestor, Joseph Willis, the first Protestant missionary to cross west of the Mississippi River just over two hundred years ago, died finally of pneumonia that was exacerbated by riding a horse in a February rain in Louisiana, traveling from one church to the next.

Who do we think we are to deserve an easier journey than they had? When God calls us, we must respond, we must try, we must risk, and we must seek to be faithful to the call as best we know how.

My work in Washington turned out to be even harder than I had imagined. Many nights in the first few months, I lay awake wondering what on earth I was doing in this city. Don't you imagine that the Apostle Paul had some sleepless nights in Asia Minor over the years, wondering what on earth he was doing in the midst of such resistance and challenge? But my sense of God's call, and my memory of seeing Jesus on the Metro, gave me courage and peace to continue.

12

LESSONS FROM THE UNDERGROUND RAILROAD

ON THE OHIO RIVERFRONT IN CINCINNATI, ADJACENT TO THE Reds' baseball stadium, is an amazing place called the Freedom Center. It is a museum commemorating the work of the Underground Railroad. The Freedom Center sits on the Ohio side of the river, right at the historic Roebling Bridge, facing south into Kentucky, into the land that was once Confederacy territory, where slavery was legal.

The Underground Railroad was a network of persons and groups (many inspired by their devotion to Jesus Christ), who worked up and down North America in the nineteenth century to transport escaping slaves from one safe house to the next all the way from the Deep South up through Ohio, and on into Canada. When a black man or woman arrived in Toronto, he or she was no longer an escaped slave, but a free person. The Underground Railroad was one of the country's earliest examples of mass civil disobedience, as thousands of Americans, both white and black, worked at some personal risk to address the greatest social injustice the United States has ever known.

For many years, it was unclear what the ultimate outcome would be from the larger movement to abolish slavery. But even in those years of grave uncertainty, many worked steadily, persistently, subversively to end the injustice of slavery by simply helping thousands to escape it, one by one. Some persons of color who could have escaped stayed behind to help others. Many white folks, at considerable personal risk, worked tirelessly to provide the safe houses and even to sneak through the woods with God's children in the middle of as dark a night season as the United States has ever known.

The Underground Railroad offers us a helpful metaphor for church as movement (as opposed to church as settled establishment). It also comes from our own heritage in North American Christianity. It belongs uniquely to North American Christians, lifting up a reminder of one of our finest hours, when the reign and rule of God came near, when, in Jesus' lingo, the kingdom of God was at hand. The Underground Railroad provided a moment of choosing. People had to choose to get on board or not, just as they chose in first-century Palestine whether or not to receive the God Reality that attended Jesus and to follow him.

In the Freedom Center lobby, a large quilt hangs on the wall, commemorating and celebrating the Underground Railroad. Woven into that quilt are four core values of the movement. These core values were not documented back then, but only in retrospect by historians. Nonetheless, each value operated powerfully within the movement. These four core values are *courage, cooperation, perseverance,* and *freedom.* I want to speak briefly to these four *movement values* because they are so critical for pilgrim people, for movement people. They are mantras that help me stay on track in my work.

Courage. Some folks have to muster extra courage to speak to a big crowd. I do just the opposite. Years ago, I became accustomed to speaking to several hundred at a time. For me, it takes more courage to stand before a tiny crowd than a large one. It is easy for me to draw energy from a full house. I have to muster energy when I am looking at a room that to me seems uncomfortably empty.

Further, I know that at any given time, at least half of the people I share with in ministry projects in D.C. will no longer be with us a year hence. We constantly live with the threat of losing one-half of our leaders and one-half of our financial support.

Two components of courage relevant to this discussion are (1) managing to do (and say) the right thing even when it promises to be difficult and (2) choosing moment by moment and day by day not to worry about what happens in response to the right thing we have chosen. Courage is thus both about taking the plunge as an act of trust in God *and* about refusing to sweat that which is out of our control. We are courageous if we are intentional about these two moves. Personally, I have found that morning prayer is *essential* to my staying focused and poised in my life and work. I must choose anew each morning to trust God and not to dwell in the black hole of anxiety. During warmer months, I sit on the roof deck of my building with a cup of coffee, a prayer journal, a Bible, and often another book from a spiritually contemplative guide. I am attempting to work as a Christian minister in the twenty-first century, and to do so far out from the settled places. Doing this kind of work without a daily spiritual ritual would be irresponsible to my health, to the people I love, to the people I lead, and to God. Sometimes, I need to stop in the early afternoon and refocus yet again, depending on what happened in the morning. Bad news in the morning can wipe a person out. For me it's very simple to know when I need to stop and take extra prayer time: when I feel my joy slipping and I am feeling discouraged, sad, angry, or tired, it is time to stop working, if only for a fifteen minute recentering break, to breathe deeply and to receive anew the Holy Spirit. Sometimes, I just need a cat-nap. Courage demands this. The person whose appointment gets pushed back will be much happier with the person I am fifteen minutes late than to experience me when I am worn down.

When we do not see progress in our work, when we are unhappy with the quality of our work, or if we feel as if we are losing ground, we may experience spiritual and emotional crisis—unless we are drawing courage anew each day from the God who called us, who gifts us and whose Life sustains us day by day. On the other hand, when things seem to be going very well, we can relax to the point that we begin to skip our daily time with God—leading us into a colossal trap—where we are outwardly thriving, but inwardly starving, losing focus, and drifting. This is a spiritual danger zone where marriages are placed at risk and where addictive behavior can take on a life of its own. In tough times and in what may appear to be easier times, a daily rhythm of prayer remains essential for all who would seek to live courageous lives for God.

Cooperation. The ecumenical movement (a movement of cooperative life between various Christian groups) gathered steam in Asia a century ago as Christian missionaries discovered that their common ground was far more significant than their differences. When working against the backdrop of traditional Asian religions that were normative in the region, the differences between Presbyterians and Methodists, for example, seemed like footnotes. During the twentieth century, in many parts of the world the ecumenical movement spawned a wave of denominational mergers. Most of these mergers in North America resulted in steadily shrinking new denominations, sometimes with a significant ideological disconnect between the national office and many of their rural and suburban congregations. Some of these new, merged groups never regained the clarity of identity and mission that characterized some of their predecessor bodies premerger. For this reason, the trend of denominational merger has slowed to a trickle.

Today the ecumenical movement is no longer reflected in a push to merge denominational structures, but more in a new spirit of collaboration between churches on the frontlines of ministry. One of our new faith communities in downtown Washington is jointly owned and sponsored by Baptists and United Methodists. My church's ministry to deaf children and their families in suburban Maryland has become a joint effort pooling United Methodist, Lutheran, and Episcopal church leadership. In neither case do we seek to create a united parish that obliterates the existing congregations and their connectedness to the Alliance of Baptists, the Episcopal Church, or whomever. We are simply partnering on the front lines of ministry as distinct churches, working side by side.

In the case of our midweek worship community, participants may come to think of themselves as (1) Baptist, (2) Methodist, (3) Metho-Baptist, (4) Christian, or (5) none of the above. They may choose to join one, both, or neither of the churches that sponsor their faith community. If, as we hope, we reach persons together on Wednesday night that we would not likely reach in either of our separate Sunday services, then this effort will be *very well worth it,* and it will advance the mission of both the Baptist congregation and the Methodist. We expect that, in time, each church's ministries should be stronger as a result, each church's financial base expanding, and our common talent pool for various mission projects deeper than before. For persons who have long been acculturated to church life, this kind of arrangement may cause some discomfort. Such partnership can be effective as long as the leaders of the respective churches work toward one another with a desire to do something together for the community that they could not do as well apart.

The small Episcopal and Lutheran churches we work with had no children, but they partnered with us when they saw that we found a community of deaf children and their parents who had no church. I have likewise gathered a handful of folks eager to roll up their sleeves in community service, to hit the streets and work with persons living in poverty. We partner with established programs and ministries where we can plug in to well-developed networks and community programs, where volunteers are needed, but where we can also learn from the accumulated ministry wisdom that has helped to form these ministries into their current state. Why would we want to reinvent the wheel or compete with another group offering nearly identical ministry to the same population? When we forge cooperative partnerships, then a very

---

MINISTRY CLUE

Is there something that your church is good at, a ministry at which you excel, and which neighboring churches could join—and even claim officially as a ministry they endorse and cosponsor? Why would we hesitate to share a ministry so that multiple churches could connect with us? Secular businesses form official alliances all the time. Why are churches so slow to do so?

On the other hand, is there an area where your church does not have the necessary resources internally to carry out a ministry, but where you might partner with a neighboring church or agency that has already developed some traction in that field?

Or is there a new frontier for community ministry that is bigger than any particular church can easily bite off, but where, by creating an alliance of churches, big things become possible?

Why should smaller churches not form intentional alliances that enable them to offer a well-rounded array of activities and service opportunities to their constituents?

■   ■   ■

---

small congregation can offer a very comprehensive ministry with an array of service opportunities one might expect in a church many times our size.

Cooperation just makes good sense for twenty-first-century churches. When looking for partners, (1) look for like-minded churches in your own denomination, (2) look for churches of other denominations that share your passion for a certain ministry, and (3) look for other ministries and nonprofits working in your community where you can jump on board to advance what they have already started. You may also (4) find individuals who are actively a part of another church, but who wish to join with you simply for the purpose of helping you accomplish a particular ministry task. By all means, take their hand, and do not make church membership a litmus test of who can serve and lead in ministry projects to your community. We need one another!

Perseverance. Watching established congregations experience rebirth may feel like watching the Grand Canyon form. It is common to see change agents work for several years before the congregational systems are transformed. If there is an older generation passing off the scene faster than the new populations are coming in, overall numerical trends may continue to head south many years into a congregational renaissance.

Long leadership tenure of effective leaders is often correlated with relative congregational health. Effective leaders in challenging contexts may spend the better part of their professional lives constantly passing up offers to make a positive career move to a growing suburban congregation.

When I came to Washington, I assumed that the value of perseverance would dictate a commitment to the Epicenter project for at least a decade. I chose to buy a home rather than to rent. In various ways I sought to put down roots, just as I had observed effective church planters do in other places. After five months, when I had only managed to gather four people committed to the project, I began to wonder about the wisdom of perseverance. Was the city not ready for what we were doing? And if so, would perseverance be ill-advised? Maybe the wise thing would be to step back, curtail the project, continue to pray, learn the territory, and build a foundation for another run up the mountain in a year or two.

Thankfully, we found a burst of forward momentum after six months and began regularly to add people into the orbit of our ministry sites. During our first year of public worship services, we never held a single service that did not attract at least one brand new person. Nevertheless, we continue to navigate ups and downs.

Perseverance isn't so much the question of how long we, as pastors, stay in our current pastoral assignments, or how long we,

---

MINISTRY CLUE

Perseverance can easily be misconstrued as persistence in holding on to ministry strategies and programs that are underperforming. Perseverance should not be attached to any single strategy or project. Rather it should be attached to the purpose behind our strategies and organized efforts.

If something is not working, give it a rest! But persevere in praying and searching and trying other ways to accomplish the purpose that drives you.

■ ■ ■

---

as laity, remain as members in one congregation. I do favor long tenures where possible, for a variety of reasons—but perseverance is about more than tenure in one place. My United Methodist forebears used to have very short tenures in any given place, often a year or two. And yet, nineteenth-century American Methodism persevered in planting tens of thousands of churches from coast to coast. Clergy families persevered faithfully, as they moved kids to new schools every year or two, without ever attaining equity in a home or piece of land. Perseverance is about hanging in there day after day, year after year, and not giving up. Perseverance is also about nurturing relationships in the faith community with people who can encourage us and help us forward when we are tired or discouraged.

Perseverance is about my commitment to the journey. At the age of fifteen, I answered a call to journey with God as a pastor wherever I was sent, and I have given my life to that task. In particular, now that I am moving into middle age, and watching times and culture change from what I knew when I started, persistence means staying in pilgrim mode. I was called to a journey, like Abraham, to a land that I did not know. I am clearly moving in that new land now, with other lands perhaps just over the next hill.

The day that I think it's okay to settle down, find a friendly church, dust off old sermons from my files and coast—that is the day that I should retire, or take a sabbatical, or find another line of work. I was not called to be a settler. I was called to a journey. And if I am no longer willing or able to persevere in a life of forward movement with God, with its risks, hard work, and constant demand for learning, then I am done.

Freedom. With any God movement, there must be a point to it all, a goal toward which we move. We can courageously hang tough together and accomplish nothing good. In fact, we can courageously hang tough together and accomplish extraordinary evil. We thus need clarity about the good place or promised land toward which we strive. In the case of the Underground Railroad, freedom is the magic word that sums up the vision of African American persons living self-determined and dignified lives that befit children of God, not any more being treated as the property of any other person.

The goal of the Underground Railroad, in a word, was freedom. Freedom is still a rich word in that it encompasses much of what we strive for in the lives of human beings and whole communities. There are other equally good words. Some churches *save souls*—and they may possibly understand that task to be more related to restoring people's dignity in this life than in making reservations for them in the next life. Other churches rarely use soul-saving language. These might place *justice* in this fourth category—as they seek to create both a faith community and a world where relationships between persons are just and respectful of the value of each of God's children. Use whichever word or words best expresses the heart and focus of what your church strives toward.

All pilgrims and all pilgrim communities need a clear and holy sense of trajectory and direction. For the Underground Railroad, this meant: Courage. Cooperation. Perseverance. Freedom.

13

Discovering the Back Side of the Mountain

Charlotte, my spiritual director, presses me to wonder aloud, "What on earth are you doing in Washington, D.C., Paul Nixon?" Running around in the dark, I mutter. Scurrying to try this and then to try that. I am God's crash test dummy in this town. Yes, but *why are you here?*

Perhaps, in a certain respect, I came to D.C. to save the world, just like the many other idealists who have moved to town with the Obama administration. I certainly came with a vision. I came to connect with the varied kinds of folks who live in this city, to discover grace with them, and to forge a spiritual community with them. I came to crack a few of the enigmas about the local culture and to find ways to connect a group of urban professionals with historic Christianity. I came seeking to do this as a mission developer working in varied partnerships with established congregations. And, in so doing, I hoped to encourage their respective development. Most of all, I came with a very keen sense of God's urging.

I left a territory where I was known and trusted, and where I understood clear models of how effective churches functioned and thrived. My choice to come to Washington was definitely the choice of a road less traveled. If I had been looking simply for a bigger church, a higher salary, or perhaps a shot at making bishop, this would obviously have been the wrong place for me.

When Jesus called each of his twelve disciples, certainly they came along with a mixture of good faith and mistaken expectations. When we see Matthew's account of Peter drawing a sword on Roman soldiers in Gethsemane, we are left asking, "What on earth was an armed man doing following a teacher who was famous for his pacifism?" Obviously there were two story lines going on in Peter's journey at this point: Peter's own storyline and God's. The same is true for all of us who embark on the adventure of following Jesus. I can hope that I was not as egocentric and misguided as Peter during Holy Week when I embarked on my own spiritual journey. But even if it turns out that I was, Peter's story yet provides me with hope that time may help me get it right eventually. Or at least more right.

There is a moment for many of us when we realize that the only storyline that matters is neither the accumulated newspaper clippings about us nor the well-manicured resume of our outward accomplishments (or our children's). Suddenly we see so very clearly that we may have been missing the real story, distracted perhaps by the growth of a financial portfolio or the accumulated accolades from whomever we look to in life for accolades. Aside from such superficiality, we may have missed the story God is writing with our lives simply because we have been distracted by another very fine story that *we* are seeking to write. There may come a day that we discover that God is writing a different story than we are writing. If so, I have news: God's story is going to prevail as the definitive narrative of our lives. Whenever and however this happens, this is a gift.

I am reminded of an incident late in the life of the Catholic mystic Thomas Merton. Merton was traveling in India, and he had settled for a season into a cottage on the Mim Tea Estate in the mountains north of Darjeeling, at the base of a certain Himalayan mountain called Kanchenjunga. One night Merton dreamed about the mountain, and then he wrote the following in his journal the next morning, November 19, 1968:

> Last night I had a curious dream about Kanchenjunga. I was looking at the mountain and it was pure white, absolutely pure, especially the peaks that lie to the west. I saw the pure beauty of their shape and outline, all in white. And I heard a voice—or got the clear idea of: "There is another side to the mountain." I realized that it was turned around and everything was lined up differently; I was seeing the Tibetan side. . . . There is another side of Kanchenjunga and of every mountain—the side that has never been photographed and turned into postcards. That is the only side worth seeing.[12]

Every mountain and every life has another side, never photographed, a side that lies apart from the public, aside from the news clippings, beyond the photo albums, away from the resumes . . . a quiet side *where only you and God can go.* From the time we were children, many of us have rehearsed our lives in terms of outward achievement. In my case, when I was young, I was always the good boy and the straight A student. Later I became the high school debater, the Phi Beta Kappa key-holder, the youngest student in my seminary, and, still later, a guy who writes books and collaborates with some of the best pastoral leaders in the country.

In Washington, I came to the other side of my own mountain. It was a fearful terrain at first. I lost sleep listening to the howling of sirens as they echoed through the streets at all hours of the night. Slowly I learned to relax in this place and, I think more significantly, *to love myself in this place*—a very different self than has been apparent in all the other places where I have lived and worked. For to love myself here meant to love myself even when my work was floundering at times. It meant to see and discover my own value to God and to others apart from a batting average.

MINISTRY CLUE

Pastors, the next time that you take a personal retreat, spend some time looking at Kanchenjunga: viewing your life not in terms of the outward achievements in each place where you have served, but rewriting your story around the following questions:

- What did I learn in each year or in each place?

- What are the two or three biggest mistakes I have made across these years? What was I thinking when I made those mistakes? How has my thinking changed?

- How has God made me a better person than I used to be? How in some respects am I not as good a person as I used to be?

- If I had it to do over again, what would I do differently—and based on this wisdom, what will I do differently in this time and in this place?

- What is the tension in the plot, the struggles that seem to drive my story? How do I see God's grace intervening to resolve this tension?

■   ■   ■

I prayed more my first year in Washington than I did in fourteen years that I lived in Florida, fourteen years where every year contained a new home run, another level of achievement in my work. Not that I failed to pray in the Florida years; I experienced a real sense of spiritual awakening there in the years 2003–04. But in D.C., I began every summer morning on the roof deck of my building with a Bible, a prayer journal, and a cup of coffee . . . looking out at the defining monuments of the Washington skyline. Almost invariably, I would leave the Bible and journal on the teak picnic table upstairs and zip downstairs and back to grab a second cup of coffee. As the Epicenter movement suddenly began to take on the sinews and flesh of real life around the first of 2008, and the roof became too cold for my morning vigil, the entries in my journal became fewer and further between. By late spring, that brief wisp of Spirit life had come and gone, our momentum had evaporated and half our people were gone. Then the journal entries grew longer again . . . and more contemplative.

You get the point: that there was another story unfolding for me beyond the ups and downs of my work. An inward journey. A journey of discovery.

Have you ever considered the possibility that your church also has another story, far removed from the well-rehearsed church history that often ends up on the webpage or in the church phone directory in which is recorded a recitation of the various real estate deals completed over many decades? It is easy to see that a series of building campaigns doesn't begin to tell the story of a faith community. Nor does a graph of the rises and falls in membership, worship attendance, and financial contributions. These statistics, like the building history, hint of a storyline, but they leave us without understanding:

- why all those people joined this church in the first place
- what they hoped to accomplish together
- what their collective fears and hopes were
- when people did experience a sense of the Holy around here
- what they did in response to those moments
- when they experienced conflict, and what that was really about
- how the church navigated such conflict
- why people left the congregation across the years: death? migration? or what?
- when they displayed courage and colored outside the lines of convention

- how the larger community's story contributed to the church's story
- what God has been teaching us here across the years
- what New Thing God is doing here that rallies us with hope and energy

Often we focus on distracting details that obscure our church's real story. We may be distracted by the fact that once we had twenty times the number of active participants as we have today—something fairly common in the downtown churches of large cities. In such cases, the most important story to discern is probably not the long slow end of some glorious era, but to celebrate the new things that are happening and the new hope that is emerging in the church's life lately.

We may be distracted by an unhealthy fixation on a certain pastor whom we loved, and who may have been gone for more

---

MINISTRY CLUE

Many church leadership teams are too ensconced in bad habits and cheap history to easily share in a meaningful conversation about their story as a people. Because of this, it might be helpful to consider:

- Bringing in a skilled facilitator, perhaps a family therapist, to lay down ground rules and enforce them as the church talks through its real story and what it means.

- Holding a series of quiet, unofficial conversations first, so that people can get some space and practice in exploring the movements of God in their history apart from those who will automatically launch into negative or distorted storylines and color the whole group with their fictions.

■   ■   ■

than thirty years now, so that we tell the story of our church as a whiny game of comparing pastors over the decades, pastors who served the church in radically different circumstances. I have known churches that seemed incapable of a coherent consideration of who they were without launching into a litany about a long-dead minister and all his successors who could never measure up.

Especially when churches begin to experience numerical decline after years of numerical growth, some very bad assumptions may be tossed around as to what is causing the change in the church's growth rate, including a knee-jerk tendency to blame leadership. Such a church may have come to rest its own self-esteem on its outward accomplishments. Its leaders may now find themselves embarrassed about or unusually defensive of their steadily diminishing flock.

No two members of your church may see it quite the same way. But if your folks have not recently engaged in a conversation about your church's story that moved beyond superficialities into an engagement with the kinds of significant issues just mentioned, it may be time to brew some coffee and to tell some stories. It may be time to reconsider where you are going, what matters most to you, and what story God is writing in the midst of your shared life.

Look to see the back side of the mountain.

14

Honoring the People You Meet along the Journey

Hospitality has been a prominent theme in each place where I have served as pastor, in each of my books, and in almost all of my local church consultations. Effective evangelism is always accompanied by a spirit and practice of hospitality. When a church exists in a socially homogeneous environment, hospitality is much easier. The more diversity there is in a community, the more likely that even our best intentions at hospitality will be misunderstood.

Inside the Washington beltway, vast neighborhoods exist where the majority of adults are single. A significant slice of our population chooses to work hard, to play hard, and even to pursue long-term relationships, and *never to have children*. Recently a single professional woman moved from a central city condo out to a suburban neighborhood in northern Virginia. One Sunday morning, she decided to find a church. Upon entering the lobby, she made an effort to mill around the coffee area so as to meet some of the people who attended this church. The people were very friendly. She was not ignored, as she would be in some churches. Yet as the friendly church people made small talk with her, one asked, "Is your husband not with you today?" and another, "How many children do you have?" The people who asked these questions meant well. However, they failed to offer effective hospitality to this woman. They assumed certain things based upon their own life experience. They inadvertently communicated the message that "you do not fit here." This is but one variation on a tale that can be told in church lobbies everywhere when folks walk into our midst whose life experience is different than the local norm.

What does it mean to honor the people whose lives intersect with ours?

First, it means that we view each person as a gift, and not simply focus on those persons who are demographically like us or seem to be hot prospects for membership in our church. In many communities, especially urban places, the vast majority of the people we meet may be from a cultural tradition quite different than the dominant culture in our church. It is very easy to begin discounting these people and treating them as less important than the ones who look and act like us.

In the ancient Bedouin culture of the Middle East, various tribes roamed across a large territory. In addition, the territory was a migratory crossroads where persons from Africa, the Arabian Peninsula, Persia, and Europe were constantly moving past one another—tribally at first, and eventually with large armies. Diverse persons would meet, their paths crossing briefly, often too briefly for long-lasting relationships. The culture of Middle Eastern hospitality emerged in such a context.

In Genesis 18 and 19, the narrative sets up a contrast between the hospitality that Abraham (the Bedouin nomad) shows to three strangers and the extreme inhospitality shown to two of the same strangers when they venture down into the city of Sodom, as the citizens of the city plot gang rape against them. Abraham honors three men whom he will never see again by treating them as gifts from God. The people of Sodom treat these men like trash, as inhuman

MINISTRY CLUE

How does your culture express hospitality toward a guest? Have you ever considered that persons from other cultures may interpret your good will in ways that are unfavorable? *Extraordinary hospitality goes beyond simply doing unto others as we would have them do unto us.* It steps inside the cultural assumptions of the other and seeks to create a place where that person can truly feel at home.

- How might this affect the way that you invite guests to church activities and worship?

- How might this affect the way that you welcome guests on-site at those activities and worship events?

- How might this affect the role and types of food and drink served?

- How might this affect the language you use and the stories you tell?

- How might this affect the way that you follow up and stay in touch with your guests after such events?

■   ■   ■

commodities to be consumed and devalued in the crassest way imaginable. In turn, God honors Abraham and Sarah with a miracle baby. Sodom is destroyed by fire and brimstone. The contrast between the behavior of Abraham and that of the Sodomites is a bit cartoonlike, but the writers of Genesis seek to drive home a point. Hospitality is a value of the highest order, a matter that cuts to the very heart of what it means to live a life that is pleasing to God.

Fast forward four millenia to the twenty-first century. What does this ancient story teach your church and mine? It teaches us that we ought to see each of the persons who cross our path as a gift. It teaches us that we are wrong to view human beings as commodities. Many churches view certain persons as prospects—a term from the world of sales. Prospects are commodities, persons viewed in terms of what they can bring to the table in a business transaction. Human beings are holy, they are gifts—and to be valued regardless of what they might offer us in return. When we view persons primarily as prospects for our church, we view them as potential financial donors and potential volunteers. Furthermore, by viewing some people as prospects, we make the subtle but significant decision to view others as nonprospects. It becomes a fairly sure bet that we will treat the nonprospects differently. We will show them less attention. We will be less likely to relate to them in a way that invites them to become *one of us.*

What if we viewed each person as a gift from God, a person with intrinsic value, a person to be honored even as we would honor God—with no strings attached? What if we were open to the things that each person might teach us, open to consider that each might bring wonderful gifts to our church other than membership? One of our partner churches in the D.C. area hosts a daily ministry to street people. Several of the street people have offered gifts back to the church other than money, volunteering, and worship attendance.

What if we were open to the possibility that persons who seemed the most unlikely candidates for membership were, in fact, the very ones whom the Spirit will lead to link their lives with us in fellowship and in serving God? In every place where I have served as pastor, I have been amazed by the unlikely collection of human beings whom God draws together as church. In every type of community, I have observed persons coming together as sisters and brothers, despite enormous social and financial disparities. In the city, the diversity cuts across ethnicity and national origins as well. As we will see in the next chapter, tribe does still matter to people. But many churches are special places where different tribes can mix to experience a measure of common ground and community.

You just can never predict who will show up at your church and who will join. You may target young folks, and old ones will show up, feet tapping to the music. You may target professional folks, and street people will show up. You may target the LGBT community, and straight people show up. You may target black folks, and Hispanics will show up. You may target liberals, and a bunch of young evangelicals show up hungry to do social justice ministry! Wise churches understand that despite the enormous power and significance of tribe in our world, God loves to assemble an unlikely crew, and thus to give us a foretaste of heaven.

So we should never discount *anyone*. Each person is holy. Each one is important. Each one is a gift. Everyone serving as a worship greeter and everyone serving on a community mission team needs to understand this principle.

In addition to viewing each person as a gift, we should especially honor those we meet who are suffering. When Jesus tells the parable of the sheep and the goats in Matthew 25, he identifies six categories of people who require special attention: people who hunger, those who thirst (which is possibly a metaphor for spiritual poverty), people who are strangers, people who are clothed poorly, people who are sick, and people who are incarcerated. In five of the six categories listed, people clearly are suffering. Being a stranger does not necessarily entail suffering. However, if the stranger is an alien in a new place, then he or she is probably suffering from loneliness.

There are two ways to interpret this parable. I don't care which way you go because either will take you in a good direction.

There is one school of thought that says that *suffering people, especially those who suffer from material poverty, should be a priority in a church's ministry focus.* When I see urban churches that grew strong by focusing ministry on serving the families of incarcerated people, for example, or by focusing ministry on serving victims of AIDS/HIV, I am reminded that God can build a great church when God's people are tenaciously giving of themselves to bless suffering people whom most of society ignores. Focus your church's ministry on particular groups of suffering people in your community, especially on those who are largely ignored by other churches and devalued by the larger society. God will bless this.

The other school of thought about the parable of the sheep and the goats reminds us that everyone on earth suffers somehow, especially when we consider the aspects of spiritual poverty that exist behind the gates of exclusive housing communities, such as the addictions, the eating disorders, the broken marriages. According to this perspective, no one type of suffering necessarily takes priority over another—it is simply important that we find out *how* the people hurt in our community and address our ministry to those hurts in a spirit of compassion and hope.

MINISTRY CLUE

The famed Willow Creek Church in the Chicago suburbs popularized a fictional couple called "Unchurched Harry and Mary." This couple was a composite of the kinds of people who lived in the neighborhoods around them. In the spirit of that classic effort of one church to focus its ministry on the people of its community, consider the following questions:

- What might Unchurched Harry and Mary look like in your church's community?

- How do they suffer?

- How can your church focus its ministry toward a certain group and yet remain open to all the people God sends to you who differ from that group?

- What danger is there in defining the market for your ministry? What danger is there in failing to do so?

■　　■　　■

One way or another, when you look closely at almost any thriving congregation in North America—any church that is making a significant impact in its community and drawing people in to share in its ministries—you will discover that they are good at relieving some kind of suffering (and possibly several kinds). You will discover that they have learned well the territory where they serve, and they know how people suffer. And they have discovered tangible ways that their church can help relieve people of some of this suffering.

Soon after moving to Washington, I walked one morning into the dry cleaners on my block. Still new in town, and seeking to make small talk with anybody and everybody, I asked the woman at the counter about a recently publicized incident where a D.C. lawyer had sued a local dry cleaner for untold millions of dollars because they lost his $400 pair of pants. NPR had covered the story as a human interest story for most of the preceding year, in part because their main headquarters was only two blocks away on the same street and the story was so bizarre.

The woman was not amused at all by my question. "Did you see him?" she asked me. Did I see whom? "Mr. _____." "Who is Mr. _____?" I asked. "The man who sued the dry cleaners . . . you passed him as you came in." She explained that the man I was asking about had actually passed me as I entered her store. She said, "We are his new dry cleaners." I was speechless. Finally I asked, "Are you scared?" (This guy had just put another dry cleaner out of business as they dealt with legal fees.) She said, "We prayed about it, and we did a little research, and we learned that Mr. _____ is an unhappy man. We learned of some of the problems in his personal life, and we decided that every time he comes in, this will remind us to pray for him." Knowing that I was a minister, she asked me if I would also begin to pray for him. I said that I would.

What dry cleaner in her right mind would serve such a customer, except a dry cleaner who is motivated by a profound love for God and a calling to take risks in the name of love? I have rarely ever been so moved by the simple and straightforward commitment of an ordinary person to take a risk in order to attend to the suffering of a fellow human being. That conversation taught me a lot about Christian hospitality and attentiveness to suffering.

I do not live in nearly as homogenous a community as the place in Florida where we added three hundred new members each year to our church's rolls. The vast majority of the people I pass on Washington's streets each day are not prime candidates for membership in my church. And yet, early on in my time in D.C., a Christian dry cleaner taught me that each person I pass on those streets is vitally important to God, and also to me. Each is a child of God. Each suffers. Each is to be honored. Each represents the possibility for transformational relationship, even if that relationship is very brief.

15

PAYING ATTENTION TO THE POWER OF TRIBE

EVEN AS I LIVE IN ONE OF THE MOST COMPLEX CITIES IN THE WORLD, where a host of different languages are spoken, there is something that strikes me as I stand on the corner of 7th and H under the Chinatown archway, watching throngs of humanity overflow the sidewalks on a Friday night: people are still traveling in their tribes.

Though we have plenty of interracial couples and interracial friendships in town (especially among the highly educated set), the norm is still Asian traveling with Asian, black teens traveling with black teens, and preppy Georgetown law students alongside others who would have fit in the sororities and fraternities to which they so recently belonged. It is easy for some to take a pot shot at churches by decrying "Sunday morning at 11 A.M. is the most segregated hour of the week." However, the more I watch the comings and goings on H Street, the more I see that voluntary segregation is just as notable outside the church—if not more so.

One of our partner churches is based one block from the street corner I just mentioned. At 11 o'clock on Sunday mornings I see several tribes gathered there, same time, same place:

first, a good number of Hispanic folks, led by a Salvadoran pastor who shares in the worship leadership, often in Spanish. Then there is a Burmese contingency that sometimes worships apart from the larger group but comes into the big room on communion Sundays. A handful of elderly white people remain, the last vestiges of several thousand who belonged to this church sixty years ago. Then there is a burgeoning group of mostly white, but multiethnic, young adult professionals who have chosen to live and to worship in the heart of the city. No one group forms a clear majority, making for a very rich cultural environment that hints at the diversity and universality that we call "the holy catholic church."

And yet, even in such a multicultural congregation, people sit somewhat organized by tribe, just as they would sit at the cinema down the street: Hispanics tend to group themselves down front near the language translation earphones, the Burmese to the left, older white folks center and right in the back half of the room, and the yuppie bunch sprinkled all about, but still typically paired with others of their ilk. In other words, even as we mix cultures in a common worship experience, people still choose to travel in close association with others who share significant affinity and common life experience.

We see the same thing in school lunchrooms, at shopping malls, at ball games, and in any other public venue where we are able to choose where we sit or with whom we travel. I don't think that this is necessarily all bad.

If we said to the Burmese group at church that they need to mix more thoroughly with the larger group and stop gathering as Burmese Christians, we would be asking them to act in a way that would dilute the preservation of their Burmese Christian culture. There has been too much of that in America, in my opinion: the loss of rich cultural heritages in favor of a bland homogenization. Why not encourage the continuation of strong and distinct tribal traditions?

What if we were to make each church in Washington a perfect blend of all the racial and economic groups in the city? Each church could then have perhaps 0.9 Burmese persons. We would lose the crisp distinctiveness of the varied churches—especially in terms of music. The gospel music would have less soul. The classical music would have too few singers to be sung well in most places. A little dab of Spanish would become (at best) nice window dressing in predominantly English services in every single place. The contemporary Christian rock music would be virtually nonexistent, due to the prideful attitude of a few older, more influential members in almost every church. If you think that church services teeter on the boring side already, try homogenizing all the churches, and you will only hasten the exodus of young Americans from organized religion, and quite a few folks my age as well. It would be a disaster.

In almost all traditional cultures, the tribe makes decisions together. When individuals in a tribe choose to convert to another religion (and culture), this often provokes enormous stress and conflict. If we study the history of Christian evangelization and expansion into Africa and Asia, we will see a repeated pattern of chiefs and key influencers deciding to follow Jesus, and a whole network of people quickly falling in behind them. Typically, if a Christian community emerges within a culture where there have been few Christians, a whole set of new symbols, traditions, and hymns will emerge that are indigenous to that culture—creating a community that rallies around a hybrid of missionary influences and homegrown culture.

What does all this mean for your church?

It means that you will not likely gain many participants from outside your church's dominant culture on a one-by-one basis. Imagine that there was a major influx of Hispanic families in the neighborhoods around the famous Ebenezer Baptist Church in Atlanta. I feel safe in predicting that Ebenezer would remain almost entirely African American in its membership. Ebenezer's

---

MINISTRY CLUE

Name the tribes, the distinct groups of people that you see in the community around your church. Think hard and list as many as you can possibly can. If you do this as a group, be sure to include some public high school students in the brainstorming—a group whose members often have a better read on the diversity of a community than anyone else.

- Which of these tribes does your church currently serve?

- Which of these tribes do other neighborhood churches serve?

- Which tribes are underserved?

- Is there a tribe of people that you feel called to serve and mix with more effectively?

- Is it possible to identify the chieftains of these tribes and to talk to them?

- What ideas do you have about bringing diverse tribes together in shared community? What challenges will need to be overcome to do so?

■   ■   ■

---

identity and heritage is deeply steeped in southern black Christianity and the struggle for civil rights.

However, what if Ebenezer were to decide to merge with a large Hispanic congregation? And then, what if the new church were to retain services in two linguistic and liturgical traditions, with some occasional exchange of preachers and musicians between the two worship communities? That would introduce new possibilities. In this (somewhat unlikely) case, two powerful tribal cultures would be choosing to partner together as Christian sisters and brothers in a sense of shared community mission, while at the same time choosing to retain strong components of their respective tribal traditions.

Why would two strong churches choose such a thing? Perhaps they might wish to pool their resources in a world where buildings and staff healthcare costs are squeezing even the strongest churches. Perhaps they might wish to ally two communities around their common interests, such as creating a broader coalition for civil rights advancement. Maybe the leaders of the two churches have prayed and feel a divine urging toward a ministry that is more embracing of diversity. Whatever the reasons, the fact remains that authentic and healthy diversity in community is most easily forged when we bring tribes together as tribes. Then the members of each tribe can enter into a new community alongside others from their heritage, alongside people who share their traditions, values, and life experiences.

Short of merging churches, two churches may decide simply to partner together in the creation of a third thing. For example, a Chinese language congregation and an Anglo congregation may decide to plant a new church together which will be multiethnic from the ground up, with authentic sharing of leadership and planning. In the new church, there may be very intentional and significant sharing of the best from each of the constituent tribal cultures that are flowing into the new church. Or, if the new church is being formed by the children of the current leader generation in the parent churches, it may be that the new church bears remarkably little resemblance to the parents on the surface. *But the cultural diversity in the new church would be possible because we are joining tribal groups rather than asking individuals to forsake their tribe to align with another.*

Short of planting a new church together, Christians of different tribes can, for example, work together on community economic and justice issues, work together to sponsor a communitywide youth ministry, work together to create multicultural worship services quarterly. In each case, the integrity of each tribe is respected even as we seek to transcend the boundaries of tribe in specific ways.

If you want a more diverse church, look for ways to connect with new cultural groups en masse, not just one by one. Consider sponsoring events that bring a considerable number of a tribe together all at once. Consider forging alliances with other organizations (churches, schools, civic organizations, community service coalitions) that contain significant participation and leadership by persons from other cultural tribes. Create situations and events where multiple persons from a neighboring tribe end up on your turf simultaneously. Be sure that you deploy persons into *visible leadership* for such events from the generation, culture, or ethnicity you seek to reach. Include these same people in leadership and planning behind the scenes. Get them to the table where they can use their life wisdom and tribal sensitivities to advise the larger group.

MINISTRY CLUE

Blended worship has received bad press in many circles in the last few years due to some very awkward attempts to include styles of music in the same service that do not flow easily together. This creates a situation where everyone is equally miserable.

However, every worship community in the world has a certain range of musical style—and most churches have some variety in their range. What is the current range of your church's musical style?

How might you expand that range? Are there additional types of music that could gracefully be added to the range of what you do in your current gatherings? Is there a constituency who would appreciate such an effort?

If your church were to add a new weekly worship gathering, how might the music in the new service fall into a different range? Who would need to be a part of a conversation about what this range would be?

■   ■   ■

Any attempt to draw varied cultures together in community should be accompanied by great care in terms of the language that we use. Words have different history and connotations with different tribes. The more diverse the community, the greater care we must give to language. This has nothing to do with political correctness. It has everything to do with respect and love for one another.

Just as we must be sensitive about words, we should also be sensitive about artistic styles employed in a diverse gathering. Please do not force-feed people of other tribes with a heavy diet of your music and culture. Such arrogance will cause your ministry to fail. At the same time, do not assume that burying or denying your church's musical taste and dominant culture is a better way. If the people of your church enjoy a certain kind of music, be sure to include that music in your church's life. Most people have limited tastes and cultural tolerance, both the people who currently attend our churches and the people who do not. We can tolerate a certain range of different tastes and sounds, but most of us don't relish a steady diet of sounds outside our comfort zone. *This is why it is sometimes better to encourage specialized worship communities and ministry groups to form around specific cultural values and tastes.* You can occasionally mix the groups or expose one group to the cultural gifts of another group, and everyone will likely have a good time! But don't expect Pentecost every Sunday. That may wear everybody out.

Tribe is a part of human life that is older than any particular religious tradition, and a part of life that will be with us until the end of time.

Think tribe.

16

GIVING THE WORLD
SOMETHING BETTER THAN
MORE CHURCH PEOPLE

THE FIRST TIME I EVER SAW MY FATHER CRYING WAS IN 1968.
I was six. I walked into our living room and found him watching
TV. I looked at the black and white screen and back at Dad. "Why
are you crying?" I asked. "A great man has died," he answered. Years
later, he elaborated to me why the funeral of Martin Luther King
Jr. moved him so deeply. Dad pastored a church in Austin, Texas,
from 1961 until 1968, a church that doubled in size and built a new
education building. In terms of how most of us were trained to
measure ministry results, it had been a good run. During this time,
the first persons of color attended that church, and he stood down
those whose racism caused them to resist black and white folks
worshiping together. It had been a genuinely good run.

And yet when King died, Dad realized that one of the great
God-movements of the ages had just occurred and he had missed
it, preoccupied with growing a congregation, raising funds, and
building a bigger facility. Imagine that you lived in Jericho on the
day that Jesus came through; but you were behind at work, and so

you chose to skip the parade and catch up at the shop. There would be no instant replay—the opportunity of a lifetime would have slipped through your fingers. Dad was not crying for Dr. King that day. He was grieving the loss of his opportunity to share more fully in the civil rights movement that had unfolded over the preceding decade. He hadn't done much or said much. The opportunity of a lifetime: missed.

Forty years later and still there is nowhere on the annual report we send in to our denomination's headquarters asking us to account for how and where our congregation discerned the reign and rule of God breaking into the world last year and what we did to get behind it. The higher-ups still are mostly interested in new church members added, how many died, how many showed up on the average Sunday, and how much money fell into the collection plates. Highly institutionalized structures that have grown up around the Christian faith sometimes cause us to measure the damndest things, and they may distract us from the most important things.

I am not at all opposed to numerical benchmarks, so long as they target things that really matter. But some of the most important things may not easily translate to institutional mathematics.

One of the aspects of my work in D.C. that I have enjoyed is my association with persons of extraordinary promise—the young economist down at the Fed working long nights through the 2008 financial meltdown, the IBM executive called to simplify his life so that he can steer more of his resources toward serving poor people, the sixty-one-year-old widow (going on thirty) on the thrill ride of her life in her second year of theological training, the twenty-year-old former gang member one year into his Christian adventure, studying filmmaking at Art Institute of Washington so that he can reach his generation with the Christian good news—and on I could go. The faith communities we are developing in our city exist to cultivate the very best in the lives of each of these persons, and to hurl them toward the stars, for the glory of God.

MINISTRY CLUE

In that focus group of persons in your community who attend no church: you might ask them to reflect with you around the following questions:

- What are churches known for in our community?

- If we were to just close all our community's churches, would we lose anything of value, in your opinion? If so, what?

- If you were named Pope, and could virtually wave a wand and change thousands of churches and make them different or better, what might you do in your first year?

In addition, explore the following ideas:

- What if the church existed simply to help human beings soar to the stars?

- What if the only measure of our success was the excellence with which we coached people to discern and to live out God's dreams for their lives personally—as parents, as spouses, in addition recovery, stress management and so forth? Would they find a place like this worthy of their time?

■　■　■

How do you measure that?

As I write this, I add up the faces from last week and they total around sixty folks. A few years back I heard someone say that they would rather have a church of sixty who were committed to becoming world changers than a church of six hundred who were committed simply to attending worship services. When I heard this, the words *cop out* immediately came to mind. I have always felt that with six hundred or with six thousand, the possibilities are amazing, even if most of the crowd is underperforming in terms of living on the ragged edge of what God is up to in the world. When I used to preach to six hundred each week in Florida, I always saw the potential in each chair. I knew that only a few would dare to step out and follow Jesus in ways that truly captured the spirit of his invitation along the shore of the Sea of Galilee. But, my goodness, what wonderful things came from the few who dared!

However, I wonder now if we might not unleash more world changers by means of a small to midsized congregation *where the challenge is high* than through a larger church where the majority of participants remain simply *consumers* of great music, entertaining preaching, and clever children's ministries. I sense that many of the would-be consumers, who are increasingly choosing *not-to-be*, might be truly interested in a place where the point was helping them to discern their purpose on the planet and to live passionately into God's dreams for their lives. (So many of the folks who have given up on church have really just given up on building a religious Disneyland.)

But how on earth do you measure this?

In the end, you can't always measure miracles statistically and scientifically. But you can usually develop good anecdotal evidence.

The slavery abolition movement seems to me to be the crowning achievement of the nineteenth-century American churches. In the early years of that century, about one in eight Americans belonged to a church. The churches grew until, by mid-century, nearly one in three Americans belonged to a church. Since the abolition movement was so closely aligned with churches, the growth of the churches tended to feed abolitionist sentiment. With the rise in abolitionism, the national political climate changed; and the ensuing conflict was horrendously violent. And yet, out of that changed political will and the ruins of the War between the States, Lincoln's Emancipation Proclamation emerged in 1863; and from there, a domino effect unleashed across the globe, virtually eliminating the institution of slavery worldwide within fifty years, except in a few marginalized, rogue places.

If we had packed our houses of worship twice as full but had failed to proclaim liberty to the captives of slavery, I would maintain that the church would have been less successful during that period of time. Sometimes the biggest victories just don't show up on the annual report!

Beyond the raw numbers of people who come to your church's events, who is on fire to make a difference on this planet? What in the world are the persons in your church on fire to change? What kinds of suffering do they intend to eliminate? What injustices do they hunger to rectify? What technological challenges do they strive to overcome? What global crises do they care about sufficiently to devote their lives to solutions?

Martin Luther King Jr. said, "The arc of the moral universe is long, but it bends toward justice."[13] Despite repeated social nightmares and genocides over the last century, I think King was correct in this statement. So how is your church—or perhaps more specifically how are *key people in your church*—helping to bend history in God's direction? How are your people learning to live as solutions rather than as perpetuations of the world's problems?

These are important questions.

There is much at stake in our world and in the lives of each person within our reach. Is that person going to live in sync with the Spirit's movement or in resistance and rebellion? At one level, a lot of people simply need to be saved from self-destructive behavior. But beyond recovery from narcissism and chemical dependency and what have you, *there is so much more to salvation in the Christian tradition.*

As I reflect on more than a quarter century of church work, I have been blessed to see hundreds of lives salvaged from severe dysfunction. But I could weep with my dad when I think long and

---

13. Martin Luther King Jr., "Remaining Awake through the Revolution," a sermon delivered at Washington National Cathedral, March 31, 1968.

MINISTRY CLUE

Benchmarks are important for any organization seeking to fulfill its mission. Every church needs meaningful and objectively measurable goals designed as way stations on our journey that confirm that we are in fact advancing toward God's vision for us.

The old benchmark of church membership growth is not as helpful a measure as some other things might be. Brainstorm with your fellow church leaders about new things to measure that might better indicate that you are truly growing spiritual giants. Think out of the box.

And then dare to hold yourselves accountable to the new kinds of measures that you imagine.

■ ■ ■

---

hard about how seldom I have helped these great people to move beyond a modest salvation and a minimal discipleship.

I just don't think we get it.

Some of our churches are so lost and confused that evangelism for them simply means getting some other folks to take over usher duty and join the finance team before our current team wears out for good. Others do understand that we exist to save souls and not to prop up tired church institutions—and yet they still see salvation in such a diminutive way, with the end goal being people who sit on our benches a couple times a month, complete some kind of Bible study program, make a hefty pledge to the church budget, and cheerfully help with the annual chili supper. We still too often reduce discipleship to being institutional church people.

Making more church people isn't necessarily going to help the world much. It may help a little. It can help especially with grief, fear, and family dysfunctions. But if all we do is make more church people, there is some evidence that we are simply creating easier prey for cynical forces to manipulate politically as they work our Olan Mills directories for their candidates and their causes. After the way that church people were used in the 2004 U.S. election, it finally dawned on me that the world doesn't necessarily need more church people.

The world needs more Jesus people. The world needs more people who are growing up to question the prejudices of their childhood, more people who are unleashing the power of compassion within their hearts and minds and communities, more people with skills at peacemaking, more people who are really able to see their neighbor and to listen to that neighbor. Is your church helping to make such people? Jesus told us to go make disciples. Are you making some Jesus people? All else pales in the light of that question.

The majority of existing Protestant congregations are going to be smaller ten years from now than at present. That is a sociological reality. Our new churches will also likely be somewhat smaller as a whole than they were in the twentieth century. However, our community and world impact can easily be larger if we more rigorously follow Jesus. In our situation, the very worst thing we could do would be to lower our expectations of the people in our churches, shrinking the level of commitment expectations alongside the decline in the numbers of people signed on with our churches. As churches raise the commitment expectations, they usually attract more people as a byproduct.

A church's leadership team can figure out if they are growing spiritual redwoods or bonsai trees.[14] If there is a widespread deepening of faith commitment, there will be evidence: amazing stories of personal transformation emerging all over the community. We could even count the number of our flock who will put in writing

---

14. Bill Easum's metaphor from his book *Growing Spiritual Redwoods* (Nashville: Abingdon Press, 1998).

a statement of personal mission and an account of what they are doing to live this out. That much is measurable, even if the full effects of their efforts are beyond our capacity to document.

When I was twenty-five, I imagined that I would look back on my career in church work and glow about how I had helped to grow the size of the congregations I served. Already now I look back on my life and glow more about the lives I challenged, and about the amazing things some of these extraordinary people went on to accomplish for the glory of God and the betterment of our world. It probably won't be the churches that I remember so fondly, but the special people who dared to live large for God. I have come to believe that the greatest measure of our impact is not the size of our church systems but the size of the vision we help cultivate in the persons who partner with us.

Can you name half a dozen or more people in your church in which you sense the presence and power of God? Are you praying for these folks? Are you cheering for them? Are you mentoring them? Are you rolling up your sleeves and helping them?

If a young man from a dusty synagogue in Nazareth can grow up and do what Jesus did, then surely God can do amazing things with the persons in your congregation. Your church's greatest contribution to God's work in the world could well be the amazing people you send from your midst into the world to serve in every imaginable capacity as dreamers, peacemakers, and world changers.

Find ways to cultivate extraordinary people for God. A church that is passionate about this will never be irrelevant.

The churches that really understand this and harness their resources and efforts to cultivate extraordinary people for God, these churches have some great days ahead! The new world belongs to such churches! The meek will inherit the earth.

How will this planet be a better place because your church was here? For God's sake, give this planet something better than just a few more church people!

17

Staying in Touch with God's Call

The concept and experience of God's call to ministry varies somewhat from one Christian tradition to the next. In some circles, there is quite an accumulated tradition of pastors and priests experiencing a tangible sense of God calling them to their pastoral role, usually at some time between their teens and their forties. In certain strains of Pentecostalism and the African American church, the call to preach is a matter of enormous emphasis. In some of the Protestant mainline groups, many clergy do not have nearly so dramatic a sense of being divinely summoned for their work.

But we know about this type of call, in part because pastors get a lot of airtime within the church in which to talk about their faith experience. Church culture thus encourages and nurtures clergy call. Ordination rituals are, in large part, celebrations of such experiences.

The concept that persons other than pastors (laity) may also receive a call from God is a much less developed idea in Christian circles. Both Catholic and Protestant theologians have given considerable attention in recent years to the idea that the sacrament of baptism constitutes a call to ministry for each of God's people. While I subscribe to this latter idea, I think baptism remains a bit generic as a call to ministry; it does not make nearly as compelling a narrative as the notion that God comes to an individual in the flux of life and mysteriously opens the door to a very specific task or way of life.

Perhaps the least understood type of call is the experience of God calling a whole group, be it a congregation, a faith-based alliance, or a denomination. Whenever a group discovers a sense of call, it typically grows out of a joint sense of vision about God's desired future. The call is rooted in the magnetism of the vision, the luring and gravitational pull of the vision.

Discovering a new congregational vision usually occurs in relationship with an influential individual (pastor, lay leader, coach/interventionist) who helps the larger group to see a new possibility. Beyond the power of suggestion, the Spirit of God then takes this new idea and causes it to germinate and take root in the hearts of the group members. The group members then begin to experience a sense of calling or deep longing to move together toward this desired future.

In my 2002 book, *Fling Open the Doors*, I recounted an experience in which seven leaders from my church in Florida spent a two-hour lunch in a small upstairs banquet room of a local restaurant with a coach/interventionist.[15] In that gathering, we simultaneously saw a new ministry possibility that none of us could see before, and we simultaneously felt a compelling attraction toward this new thing. In two hours, our church went from being utterly puzzled about our future to receiving what we believe was a clear call from God to buy thirteen acres of land eight miles from our church's property and to build a second facility that would function as an additional ministry campus for our church. I know that

15. Paul Nixon, *Fling Open the Doors: Giving the Church Away to the Community* (Nashville: Abingdon, 2002).

sounds amazing, but "call stories" are often quite amazing. Just a few years later, having followed this call with due diligence, that church was gathering a thousand people a week at the new campus for weekend worship gatherings and several hundred other people a week for a variety of other church and community activities—all this while the original campus continued to bustle with life.

When the going gets rough, it is very helpful to remember and to reclaim the vision God has given us, and God's call to us to lead and move in a certain direction. I try to imagine what my experience in Washington would have been if I had not come to the city with a clear sense that God sent me here, with a clear vision of God's Reality that we were working toward, and a trust that God was with me in that work. I imagine that it may have been an experience of despair.

MINISTRY CLUE

When, if ever, have you had an experience such as finding Jesus on the subway? When was the last time that something occurred in your life that took on holy meaning and offered you a renewed sense of what to do?

If you come from a highly rationalistic background, thinking theologically about your life experiences may not come easily for you. Meaningful moments in life do not have to be bizarre or outlandish or magical. God speaks to people through very ordinary events and experiences.

Think about the biggest decisions you have made in life, decisions related to your faith, your work, or your family. Was there a moment of internal clarity that came to you prior to those decisions? Where was God in that moment?

You might find it helpful to write down such experiences and to save the writing in a place where you can read it again occasionally.

■　■　■

During the last year, I read the autobiography of Dorothy Day, the founder of the Catholic worker's movement. She titled that book *The Long Loneliness*, referring to that season of her life when (almost a century ago) she was new to town in New York City, without friends yet, and struggling to make ends meet. Day's long loneliness became a metaphor for both the experience of urban alienation as well as for the experience of being on a life adventure apart from an awareness of the presence of God. Dorothy Day was an adventuresome spirit from her youngest days, exploring all kinds of people, places, political movements, and ideas with brilliant abandon. And yet beneath the romantic surface of her early life, there was a profound loneliness.[16]

For all the disorientation of my early months in D.C., I never experienced such loneliness. When Christ called his disciples to scatter across the Roman Empire, he promised to be with them until the end of the age. We never have to experience abject loneliness when we are on a mission adventure with the Spirit of Christ.

I did experience loneliness briefly in my first full-time pastoral assignment in a small town near Dallas. In that instance I was thrown into a town where I was a sociological misfit, one of the few adult males in town who had been to college, let alone done graduate work. I began to despair and to wonder if I was in the right profession. A good therapist, the careful reclamation of my sense of God's call, and Paul's second epistle to the Corinthians helped me to pull myself together in that place. I discovered that I was not alone at all. I had been called.

Moreover, I had been *sent* to that little Texas town, and for reasons that certainly eclipsed my own agenda and imagination. I recall visiting with my bishop about halfway through that challenging pastoral appointment, communicating my deep sense of discouragement, and then visiting with him again about five

16. Dorothy Day, *The Long Loneliness* (New York: Harper and Row, 1952).

months later—when he commented, "I am pleased and somewhat amazed how much better you are doing." The church was not thriving, but now I was. In my second year there, I found an inner peace and calm that was helpful in the chaotic environment of a town and church in an economic depression. Life and ministry have thrown all kinds of challenges at me since that time, but I have never felt undone, in large part because I learned in that first tough place how to care for myself and to depend upon God. For pastors, both self-care and the practice of trusting God begin with us regularly revisiting the divine calling that set us out on our ministry journey to start with.

No pastor, no servant of God, no community of faith can live well without a vision of God's desired future and clear sense of call from God to head in that direction.

I have experienced a call from God at various points across the years, in 1977, in 1981, in 1989, in 1996, and in 2006. The last experience (in the D.C. Metro, recounted earlier in this book) was as notable as the first. No two were alike, and yet each was connected, building upon earlier experiences. I used to think of these episodes as mini-conversion experiences. And they have indeed each functioned as doorways to a deeper trust of God. However, when we think of a conversion experience, we are usually talking about a beginning point on a conscious faith journey. So thinking of these occasional moments as divine markers on a continuous journey, rather than conversion moments, is probably better and less prone to misinterpretation.

I have been deeply influenced and spiritually formed within a Wesleyan theological framework, where we place great emphasis on the Christian life as a growth process. I am thankful for such a tradition that has cultivated in me openness to the experience of God's call. But all of us who are a part of the Christian movement find our spiritual roots in the biblical narrative, which contains scores of instances in which God calls people and groups of people into relationship and into purpose and mission.

MINISTRY CLUE

Has the leadership team at your church experienced a sense that God was calling them, indeed calling your church, to move in a certain direction? Ask around. Invite old-timers to share their memories. To the degree that anyone can recall such a moment and experience, it can be an enormous resource for your leaders today as you again wait for God to unite you in a sense of holy consensus.

As we consider the past to discover the patterns and wonder of God's presence and work among us, it is important to *look beyond the personalities and leaders of that time*, since so often we practically beatify them and inadvertently devalue the present team of leaders.

Helpful questions for consideration:

- How did our leaders feel puzzled or intimidated by the church's situation back then?

- What was the essence of our church's prayers during that puzzling moment?

- How did God answer those prayers?

- Do you remember the moment when you had a moment of discovery as to where God was leading the church?

- What about that experience would be helpful for us to recall today?

■ ■ ■

I do not recommend embarking on any significant or risky journey with God apart from the clear sense that *God has called you* to travel in a certain direction. Spiritual journey apart from God's vision and calling is just going to end up lonely and frustrating. You may get so burned out by the process that you end up angry and estranged from God. Many times, I have watched this happen to people who were too headstrong with God, who basically *called themselves* to serve God in a particular respect. There is absolutely no joy to be found in life when we try to make all the calls.

If you personally have experienced a vision and call from God, hold on to that word and that direction as a compass for your journey. Revisit that experience regularly in your memory and in your praying. If you cannot identify a clear call from God, I encourage you to take some time to wait and to listen. Jesus took a symbolic forty days at the outset of his public ministry in order to carefully untangle his own ego from the purer God impulses moving through his soul. He took time to be still and to reflect, averting what could have been a mediocre and quite self-indulgent life.

If your church's leadership team has not recently experienced a sense of clear vision and a moment of calling from God toward that vision, why not postpone making a huge decision until your leaders can find some sense of consensus about where God is calling your church to go and what God is calling your church to do? I am a believer in the urgency of now, and I know that most churches procrastinate doing what they need to do. However, if you rush wholesale in a certain direction without spiritual clarity, then when the road gets tough some of your key people may leave the church in fatigue or begin blaming others in leadership, creating dissention.

Consensus does not require unanimity, but it does mean that the *vast majority of the group is at peace with one another,* choosing to trust one another, and earnestly watching and listening together for God's direction, open to embrace a common direction and plan that is faithful to God's urgings and compelling to most of the group members. After you sense a direction from God together, your polity may require you to confirm it by voting. Some church developers discourage voting. Personally, I think that voting makes for a clean transaction, where each person is able to remain honest in the process of group decision-making. However, if a group of church leaders cannot find at least a 3 to 1 consensus around any

decision of major significance, I would urge caution about pro-
ceeding—especially if the issue comes with a fund-raising price
tag. Trying to execute big decisions with a 52 to 48 vote is often the
prelude to a church split. Occasionally, we have little choice but to
take a close vote and to proceed—but I simply urge caution.

Often, a quiet, prayerful, respectful conversation can help a
conflicted group discover an alternative way that can garner more
widespread support. In such conversations, we listen and watch
for the gentle urgings of God's Spirit. To the degree that any
group, even with a history of conflict, can experience a common
sense of God's fresh call, they usually can rally around this experience and make some very helpful and positive decisions about
their ministry and common life.

The call of God is like oxygen to the enterprise of doing
church. We cannot thrive long without it.

18

TRUSTING GOD
THROUGH IT ALL

FINALLY, A JOURNEY WITH GOD IS A JOURNEY OF TRUST. THERE ARE many biblical tales of trust on the journey with God. In both the Israelites' epic journey through the wilderness and the ministry journey of Jesus and his disciples, we see a purposeful relationship between God and a community of faith. In both cases, there was simply no way for the community to travel carrying along adequate provisions for life. The community was required to trust God for miraculous provision that was then provided in utterly unexpected ways along the journey itself. In either case, obsession with money and financial security would have left the potential pilgrim either to stay in Egypt or to keep his day job in Capernaum. Despite false starts and tragic missteps, the Israelites and, later, the apostles learned to practice trust in God. In either case, the failure of God to provide would have left them starving. Profound trust in the provision of God thus became one of the most fundamental aspects of spiritual journey in the biblical tradition.

Trusting God has much to do with our attitude toward money and material provision. Indeed, the love of money is the root of all evil. Clinging to money feeds our resistance to trusting God.

Such trust is no easier today than it was in biblical times, and no harder. Along my own journey, I wondered a few times in the early days if I would get paid my salary on time. But, honestly, I always knew I would get paid eventually, and I knew exactly how much. The Bible people didn't have that safety net. Nor did they often have affluent relatives or any larger social safety nets.

One simple way that I have sought to exercise trust in God is that I have given away one out of every ten dollars I have earned since I was ten years old.[17] I did this in graduate school when my income was below the poverty level. And I have continued to do this in later years, when I made considerably more money, but as I juggled the need for building up college savings accounts and paying off unexpectedly large tax bills. I have never missed a meal, a car payment, or been placed in special hardship for lack of that 10 percent in my bank account. Very minimal faith has been required for me to continue this practice, since my parents trained me to do it.

There is no across-the-board rule or concrete theological mandate that demands one tenth of my income as a contribution to God's work in the world. In terms of tithing, I know that I am adapting an ancient practice to my life context. Tithing was born from an ancient Hebrew community's need to store up grain in order to help destitute people and to enable everyone to survive occasional famine. It is quite a leap from that context to say that I owe God one tenth of my money in a twenty-first-century society. In fact, the teaching of Jesus would suggest that God asks for much more than that. The biblical teaching on the tithe probably relates just as much to the need (in our time) for an adequate tax code to create a decent social safety net.

---

17. When I talk about giving money to God, I mean money given to churches, charitable organizations, humanitarian causes, and other people, beyond our families, who have special needs. People ask if a tithe should be calculated on income before taxes or after. I reply, "Pray about it and do whatever seems best." It is not a legal requirement, so why be legalistic? The point for me is not legalism, but stretching myself in manageable and measurable ways to trust God.

But it has always seemed to me that giving away a tenth of my income was a good thing to do. And for whatever good has been funded with that money, I know that this discipline, practiced across several decades, has taught me more about what it means to trust God than any other practice of my life.

Giving away money when we have bills and "needs" or giving away a whole Sunday when we have work piled up from the preceding six days—this is crazy behavior! Such behavior might seem irresponsible, even lazy, from a secular point of view. And most of what we have today, even among church people, is a decidedly secular point of view. Only a very few Christians give God a tithe of their income and not many more know how to take a real day off.

But I remain a staunch advocate for encouraging people to base their charitable giving on a percentage commitment and to take a full day off each week even when they feel they need income from working a seventh day. I want my church to help folks take steady steps toward a life of trusting God.

Most of us have heard the stories and anecdotes from the lives of people who behave in such a manner: the ones who dare to go home and stop working after fifty hours a week or who dare to share with their neighbors in need when they are also experiencing financial crisis. Each of their stories seems to reveal that life somehow works better when we trust God and live graciously, when we work and spend only to a point before we stop and trust God with the outcomes.

If a church does not yet have a group of leaders who are daring and learning to trust God personally in tangible ways—including trusting God in the use of their money and their time—then we will not likely find a leadership team in that church who knows how to trust. It is unlikely we will do much better in terms of managing the church's life than we are doing in managing our own.

Local church leaders often claim lack of money as a limitation and an excuse for inaction. Money, however, is never the main issue; it is simply an easy excuse. Lack of volunteers is the next most common excuse I hear. However, the actual thing that holds churches back when God is calling them forward is lack of trust:

- When I see a church refusing to budget one dollar more than is pledged by donors even when they may historically collect $1.20 for every dollar that is pledged, I see a church that has trust issues.
- When I see a church that insists on delaying an urgent construction project so that they can save up and pay cash for the construction in a few years, even at the risk of missing growth opportunities that will be gone in a few years, I see a church with trust issues.
- When I see a church afraid to try new ministry strategies that are working well in other places simply because they tried something similar twenty years ago and it failed, I see a church that is low on trust.
- When I see a church that will not direct at least one tenth of its regular budget income to mission causes beyond local housekeeping (buildings and payrolls), I see a church that is afraid to trust God.

In each of the preceding cases of low trust, leaders have likely adopted a scarcity mentality that assumes the church has highly limited resources. A scarcity mentality is something beyond merely a disposition for conservative financial management. A scarcity mentality fails to acknowledge that the God who leads us is unlimited in resources. A scarcity mentality fails to acknowledge that God knows of other potential income streams, other potential members and donors, and other potential income even from our current base of donors as their faith increases.

I have worked with churches all over North America, and I have never yet seen a church thwarted for lack of funds—even in a bad recession. I have seen churches thwarted for many other reasons, each of which can impact cash flow, but ultimately, money is never the issue. Trust is always the real issue.

We may need to organize ourselves creatively in light of tough financial realities, even to lay off staff or to look for offbeat revenue streams to help our church fulfill its mission. Monetary challenges may well affect the ministry strategies we choose, but such challenges will never thwart the purposes of God. If we think that lack of resources is keeping our church from doing what God is calling us to do, we fool ourselves. When God provides the will, God will always show us a way.

Some of the most effective churches in the world are in Africa and Southeast Asia. There isn't a lot of money in those places. But their lack of money does not stop them from transforming families, villages, and nations. They trust God, and when God calls them to a certain path, God always shows them a way to fulfill that calling.

Your church probably has more resources than almost any of those remarkable churches in third world settings. And if your church is in North America, even if you are made up of poor people, you are surrounded by a wealthy culture with deep pockets. *As the boy learned when he entrusted Jesus with his lunch of two fish and five loaves, there were other resources on the hillside that day besides his lunch.* I don't know where all the food came from that God used to feed the thousands of people that day, but it came from somewhere. God always shows us a way to fulfill what God calls us to do.

Our job is to trust, and to give, and then to trust some more.

And then, finally, our job is to show up. Trusting God finally requires us to show up for duty. We can give generously and dream imaginatively, but finally we need to show up in ministry to people.

When I was starting out in pastoral ministry, I often wondered (during worship) if the right words would come to my lips when I stood to speak before a crowd. I remember the butterflies in my stomach on many Sundays as we sang the hymn before the sermon. One of the most amazing and oft-repeated surprises of my early years in this work was walking up to a pulpit, so very afraid I had nothing of worth to say, opening my mouth, and the words rolling out just fine. My early philosophy about preaching emerged from such experience as a two-fold discipline: (1) to do my homework (studying, praying, writing, and so on) and then (2) to show up. Often I felt that the sermon that I was serving for dinner was no gospel feast, but more like peanut butter and jelly. Afterwards, I was always amazed at what God was able to do with peanut butter and jelly.

In more recent years, I have discovered that the peanut butter and jelly principle relates to issues far beyond preaching, and beyond individual ministry tasks. We, the people of God, together may find ourselves a bit intimidated by the daunting task of connecting with and serving the changing community around us. But some things are no different today than in times past. The same God who blessed the boy's first-century fishes and loaves and Paul Nixon's twentieth-century peanut butter and jelly is still with us, before us, behind us, and all around us. Let's do our homework: praying well, learning all we can, and giving generously. And then by all means, let's show up!

The worst thing that we can do in changing times is to decide to withdraw from community and stop showing up in ministry. Too many churches, when they begin to feel puzzled about the people around them, throw up their hands prematurely and act like a church entering hospice care, sometimes thirty years before they die! Please do not do that.

Let's trust God and show up. If first efforts do not work as well as we hoped, let's learn from them and keep trying. Let's find a good way to connect with people in our community, a widely perceived community need where we can stand with folks in solidarity and compassion. Let's show up with the gifts we have—and offer to God the opportunity to multiply and to bless what we bring to the world in ministry.

Epilogue

AN ITALIAN SAILOR NAMED CHRISTOPHER COLUMBUS EMBARKED on a momentous journey in his early forties, after impressing the queen of Spain with a scheme to establish a water route to the Orient, and thereby to give Spain an advantage in the European spice trade. He made four trips across the ocean in less than a decade. Despite his beliefs to the contrary, Columbus never reached Asia. Because of severe miscalculation of the earth's circumference, he did not even come close. And Spain did not find a shortcut to India for hauling home spices.

Thus, in terms of both his personal goals and those of his investors, Christopher Columbus died a failure. And yet, he inadvertently discovered something enormous: a whole hemisphere that most of Europe did not know existed. He was not the first European to bump into America, nor would he be the last. But bump into it he did, and that discovery proved literally to be more important than "all the tea in China."

I am neither the first nor the last missionary adventurer in the United States to bump up against the unyielding presence of a new reality that lies between us and our attempts to serve and evangelize the people of our nation. I knew the world was changing before I left for Washington in 2007, and much of my earlier work focused on helping the church to navigate a steady stream of social change. But I did not understand how deep and profound the change would be.

A few of my congregational development colleagues watching various barometers had begun to suggest that an unprecedented shift was occurring in American culture in its relationship with organized Christianity. But I did not get it yet. I did not yet comprehend that the majority of the young people who had sung in my church's 120-voice youth choir in the mid-1990s were about to leave organized Christianity, possibly for good. I assumed they would become less active during their college years, but I also figured that we would be able to reach them in much the same way we reached their parents—with a new wave of programmatic innovation, some edgy music, and a good children's ministry.

I didn't get it. Not yet. It took journeying into the heart of a city like Washington for me to begin to get it.

I came to D.C. to birth and develop a church: an urban church, a theologically progressive church, but a still a twentieth-century church. Yes, it was to be multi-site and multi-ethnic, but still the idea stood fundamentally within the paradigm of best practices from the late twentieth century. Then I hit something that I hadn't counted on, standing between me and that goal, between me and the spices of Asia. Despite some great projects launched, the thing I came to this city to plant simply would not plant in the way I had expected to plant it. I puzzled for a while, wondering whether something was suddenly wrong with me. Eventually I realized that I was the same guy as before. It was simply that the world was changing, and I had come to a city—and a particular demographic in that city—where we were witnessing the forefront of those changes.

I noted that a few evangelical churches in the D.C. region continued to thrive along with some strong Catholic parishes, even in one of the most politically liberal cities in America. I marveled that these very tradition-bound expressions of faith were still finding Sunday crowds, even though our overall population was becoming so extremely secularized and individualized. But then I began to see that my evangelical and Catholic neighbors, each in their own ways, were playing well to a dwindling remnant of a Christian subculture that had once comprised more than half our nation. I came to D.C. to serve and reach a much wider population, including those who had never had a positive experience with organized Christianity. I came to work with the people who would never be caught dead walking into an evangelical church.

I found the hardest soil I had ever touched.

I am so thankful for this serendipitous journey. Because in the end, what I am discovering will certainly be more helpful to my future work as a servant of Christ than had I managed to create another twentieth-century church in a twenty-first-century city. Maybe my experience will be helpful to your journey also. I am seeing a new world—and the people of God had better take careful account of it.

As I meet people in Washington, I find myself listening to recent confirmands who now are deeply disillusioned with Protestant Christianity, some of them now agnostics and atheists. They tell me things about the state of the church that part of me would rather not know.

In addition to what they teach me, there are some people who are choosing to join with us, some of whom are coming to a new experience of faith—and each of these constituencies teaches us something valuable about the world that is coming. In the remaining years of our lives, and in the years that stretch beyond, deep into this wonderful and mysterious century, we must seek new ways to do church. By God's good grace, we shall.

We will move far beyond the boxy constraints of yesterday's models, even as we preserve the essence of a faith and tradition passed down to us by many generations of saints. I believe that we will find a way to engage in authentic and holy dialogue with neighbors who live beyond the bounds of our faith communities and beyond the bounds of our worldview. We will search for ways to bear witness to the hope that persists within us without coming across as arrogant or militant. We will learn a new rhythm of give and take, of bold witnessing and skilled listening. We will give our lives in the quest to connect the wisdom of Christ's Way with the social, economic, and environmental crises of our time. We will discern those aspects of our culture's common wisdom that overlap with our faith convictions, so that we can work together with diverse allies. A truly remarkable journey lies ahead. This will be an amazing century in Christian innovation and in the rediscovery of that critical spiritual essence that is essential to every Reformation. It is a wonderful era in which to be alive!

I confess that, right now, I am wandering a bit in the dark. We are wandering a bit in the dark, all of us—liberals, evangelicals, and everyone in between. But we wander with God. I believe that still. We wander with the One who sees over and beyond the dark fog of our current wandering. And for this reason ours is a holy journey and a journey pregnant with the possibility that we, at any hour, and in the most unlikely place, might discover the Risen Christ . . . even on the Metro in the D.C. rush hour. What matters most in a season such as this is our persistence on the journey: showing up with God, morning by morning, ready to travel another day.

We show up. We keep catching the train. And along the way, we do what we can to be faithful.